D1117887

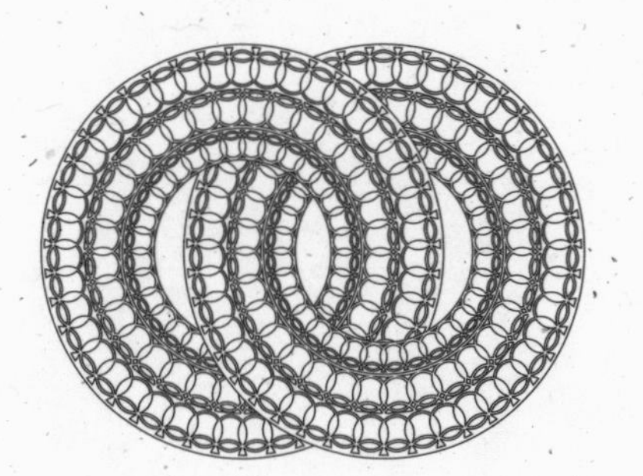

PLACES WE RETURN TO

PLACES WE RETURN TO

A Celebration of Twenty Years Publishing Fine Literature by CavanKerry Press

2000–2020

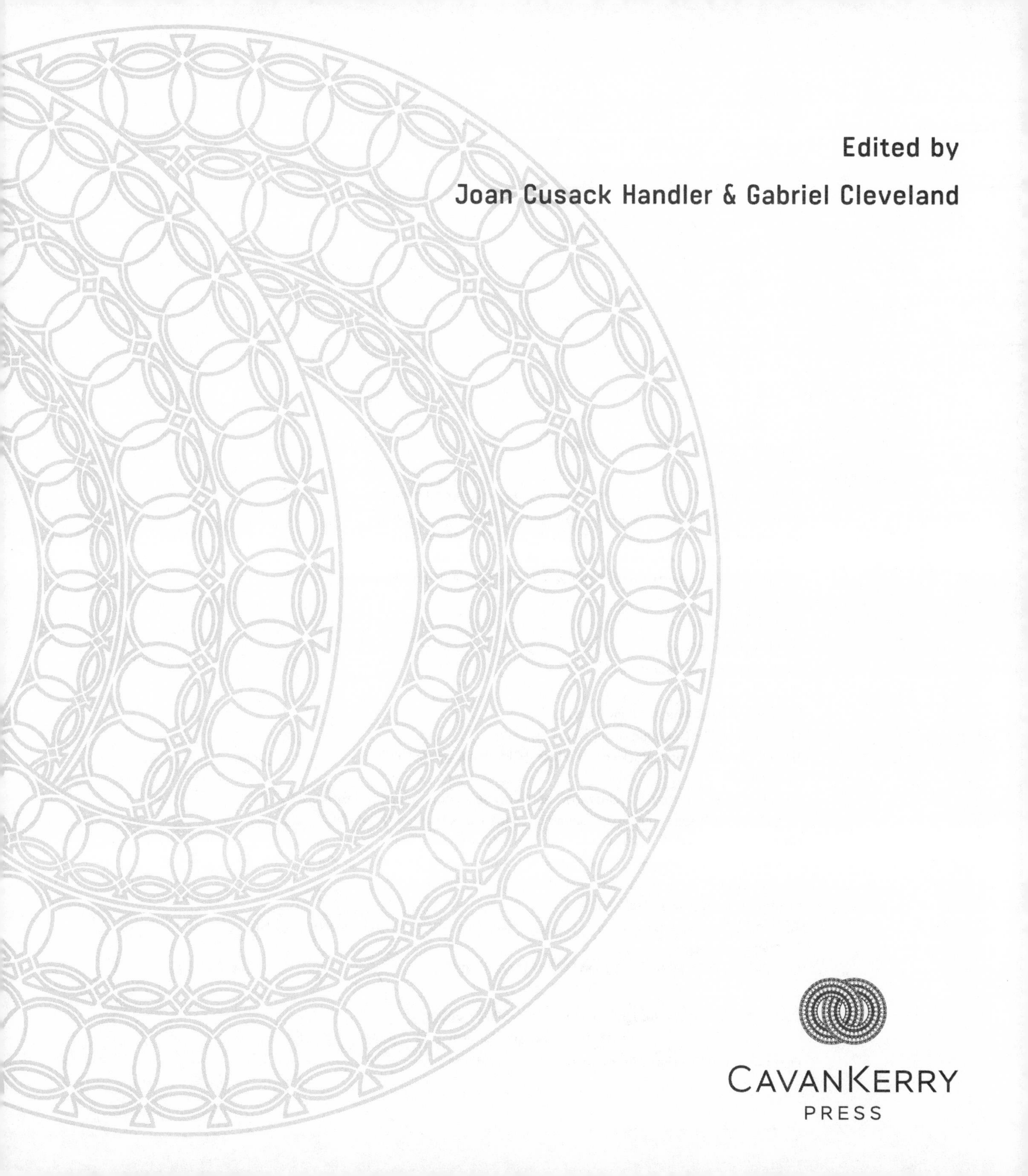

Edited by

Joan Cusack Handler & Gabriel Cleveland

CavanKerry Press

CavanKerry Press Ltd.
Fort Lee, New Jersey
www.cavankerrypress.org

Publisher's Cataloging-In-Publication Data
(Prepared by The Donohue Group, Inc.)
Names: Handler, Joan Cusack, 1941- editor. | Cleveland, Gabriel, editor. | CavanKerry Press, publisher.
Title: Places we return to : a celebration of twenty years publishing fine literature by Cavankerry Press : 2000-2020 / edited by Joan Cusack Handler & Gabriel Cleveland.
Description: First edition. | Fort Lee, New Jersey : CavanKerry Press, 2020. | Includes bibliographical references. | Summary: Contains excerpts from each of the first 104 books published by CavanKerry Press.
Identifiers: ISBN 9780967885636
Subjects: LCSH: CavanKerry Press—Catalogs. | American poetry—21st century. | LCGFT: Poetry. | Excerpts.
Classification: LCC PS586 .P53 2020 | DDC 811/.608—dc23

Cover and interior text design by Ryan Scheife, Mayfly Design

First Edition 2020, Printed in the United States of America

CavanKerry Press is grateful for the support it receives from the New Jersey State Council on the Arts.

Art is an organ of human life,
transmitting one's reasonable perception into feeling.

A real work of art destroys, in the consciousness of the receiver, the separation between oneself and the artist.

—Leo Tolstoy, *What Is Art?*

CONTENTS

EDITORS' NOTE

This anthology opens with the first CavanKerry Press book published, Howard Levy's *A Day This Lit*, which appeared in fall of 2000, and continues with all other excerpts through fall of 2020 in chronological order of their release; thus, poems appear next to memoir excerpts and essays. While we entertained the idea of separating poetry from prose for grace in reading, we decided that following our actual publication order would also tell the story of CavanKerry's growth.

Some excerpts, especially the prose excerpts, have been abridged. We have opted to not include ellipses or other distracting markers of what's been omitted in order to make them as easy to read and enjoy as possible.

Also, please note that *We Mad Climb Shaky Ladders* was published as authored by Pamela Spiro Wagner. She has since changed her name to Phoebe Sparrow Wagner. We have used her present name throughout the volume.

FOREWORD

Dear Friends,

The collection you hold is a gift book. A gift to CavanKerry and ultimately a gift to its readers.

Most importantly, it is a gift to the CavanKerry writers who entrusted their manuscripts to us to do the sacred work of transforming them into fine books and art pieces. Without them, there would be no CavanKerry.

Nor would there be this celebratory book if it were not for a handsome donation from Susan Jackson, CavanKerry poet and author of *Through a Gate of Trees*. Susan asked that we use the gift for a program or event that would honor her late mother. I was/am humbled! Susan was entrusting us with the task of creating a fitting tribute to her beloved mother. How gratifying for us that she trusted CavanKerry with such a profoundly intimate and holy task!

I wanted this tribute to be something that Susan and I would choose together. We spoke of memorializing her mother by dedicating one of our upcoming titles to her. We spoke of an event that might celebrate CavanKerry's twentieth anniversary. Finally, Susan proposed a book to celebrate our history. I mentioned that I had dreamed of creating a retrospective anthology of work from all of our 100+ books, but it was beyond CavanKerry's reach financially because we were already in the process of publishing our full commitment of books for the year. Susan loved that idea. I was overjoyed.

The first step was to enlist Gabriel Cleveland, CavanKerry's Managing Editor, a gifted editor, to share this work. We'd include one piece of poetry or prose from each of our books. Gabe asked the writers to name five favorite pieces from their books, and those we didn't have author preferences for, I reread and sent Gabe several choices from which he made preliminary selections.

Following that, we chose the final pieces. It was an inspiring collaboration for both of us.

When we began the project, the COVID-19 pandemic was barreling its way across the globe. To combat it, mandatory quarantine was instituted. For months, we were instructed not to go out of our homes except for food or in an emergency.

How does one fill those days? We started to read. And read. And read some more. Such joy to meet these poems, memoirs, and essays again! I was falling in love for the second time with the masterful, emotionally driven work that CavanKerry has published.

Despite the anxiety and terror that accompanied the pandemic, I was whisked away for several hours daily to an idyllic healing place—one filled with poems and prose pieces published by CavanKerry, in some cases, as many as 15 to 20 years ago. Such affirmation, such nourishment!

All gifts. Offered by our writers. Gifts we accepted with pride and assurance that we'd make the same decision all over again many years hence. The gift of this collection from a CavanKerry poet who wanted to memorialize her mother —a gift to savor as CavanKerry continues to mature into the soulful lover/publisher of fine literature that she is destined to be.

Happy 20th anniversary, CavanKerry Press!

Blessings and good health to all of you, our readers and friends, to Susan and her late mother, to our extraordinary writers! We are ever grateful to you.

—Joan Cusack Handler, Coeditor, Publisher

~

In Loving Memory
of
AWRG
June 17, 1917–April 19, 2011

HOMAGE TO MY MOTHER

Some of my earliest memories are of my mother reading. She sat silently, absorbed in her book, sitting by the fireplace in a wing chair that is now in my writing room. She read aloud to my sister and me before bed, on the porch in the quiet of summer afternoons, during long car rides north to visit my grandparents. My first memory of how a poem unfolds is linked to the sound of my mother's voice.

She graduated from Smith College with a degree in art history. This fascination fueled her desire to travel, to see firsthand the art and architecture she had studied in the classroom. These trips were bound up with her generosity of spirit and desire to share . . . I can see us now standing in the Louvre in front of the *Winged Victory of Samothrace* as she told us stories about the gods and goddesses of Greek mythology.

Her curiosity and appreciation of beauty felt unlimited as she took us on long walks through the Connecticut woods naming the trees and wildflowers and talking about the fragrances unfolding around us from honeysuckle, primrose, mountain laurel. There was laughter and a sense of discovery coupled with the wonder that words offer.

It is an honor to commemorate my mother's love of books along with Joan's vision for CavanKerry Press by creating this celebratory anthology. Mother would have loved it.

Susan Jackson

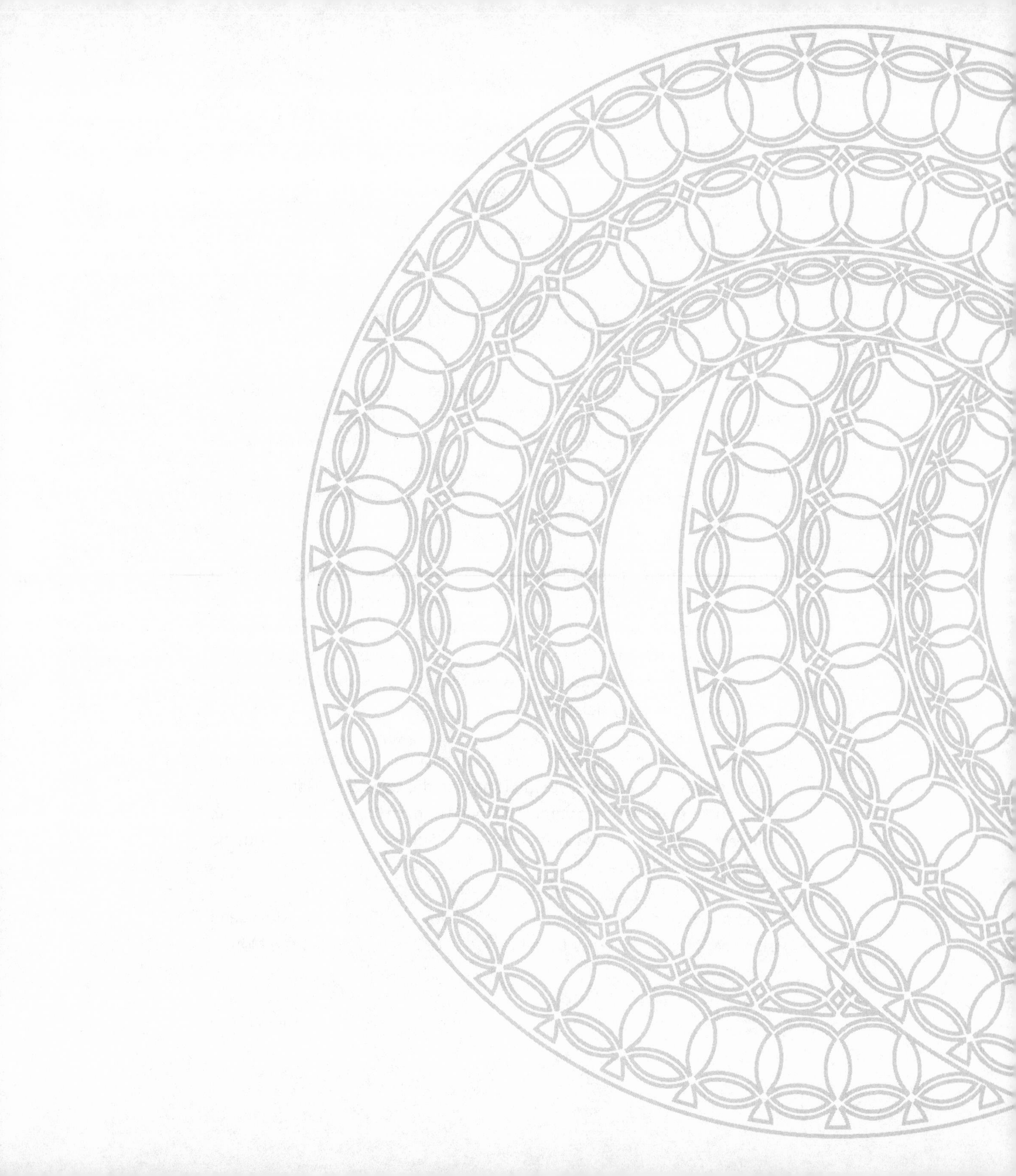

~

In grateful recognition of the writers
who entrusted CavanKerry with the sacred task
of transforming their manuscripts into fine books and art pieces,

&

in loving memory of Florenz Eisman, Managing Editor of CavanKerry Press
from its inception to her passing in 2013.

PLACES WE RETURN TO

A Day This Lit, by Howard Levy

JACKSON, MISSISSIPPI, 1966

for Shaun Griffin

When she suddenly said "Jump," holding on
to the old woman's hand, not letting go at all
though the woman was anxious to get away
from us, the trouble we brought, the mixing up
of settled things, the warm February air
of Mississippi seemed to me to collaborate,
to sustain our white college boy
arms and heads higher and longer than possible.

Mrs. Carolyn Williams, two hundred pounds if a one,
just back to her native Jackson
after the poison of Chicago, grown huge
with her appetite for change, knew
this one would never register to vote,
70, a retarded daughter in tow, scared
even by a knock at her door,
one Negro woman, two white men,
since white folks on her dirt street only meant pain
or viciousness, the bill collectors or the police,
but still deserved a treat, a gift of a moment from the future
and a joke on the rotted past.

And so when the old woman asked which of the two white men
was in charge, Mrs. Williams just turned to us
and commanded "Jump" and we jumped:
the Red Sea didn't part, the Confederate
flag didn't come down from the gold-domed Capitol
and what changed was just enough in the woman's eyes
and Mrs. Williams released her.

Kazimierz Square, by Karen Chase

THE SWIM

Still she has her silent say.

I swam nude in a creek with my mother once,
we kept a distance.
Then she said how nice I looked. Sun

on her dark hair, wet curls on her neck,
she painted cadmium red canvases. My flesh

cushions my bones, when will we get over
her drawn-out death? That creek has filled

with thawed snow, her lilies are beginning
to bloom, the sky now is begging for notice.

So Close, by Peggy Penn

MAY EVENING

some of us trim
the lawn
some of us look
for our wallet
some of us wipe
the dishes
some of us
walk the dog
some of us
have a bone scan
some of us yawn
and check our watches
some of us
have radiation
for the second time

in the cities
may blossoms fall
on concrete sidewalks
wondering
what's the next step

on a day I remember
warm then as now
a day like body temperature

a forlorn wind
stirred the leaves
buds still tight
and white green

I heard a car door

slam
they are going somewhere
without me
a punishment

I am going
somewhere too
sitting in my window
and never coming back

Carolyn Kizer: Perspectives on Her Life & Work, edited by Annie Finch, Johanna Keller, & Candace McClelland

FROM RE/MEMBERING THE GODDESS: CAROLYN KIZER AND THE POETICS OF GENEROSITY, BY JUDITH EMLYN JOHNSON

Since the late 1960s I have been slowly feeling my way toward some definition or description of a poetics of generosity, to be to our apparent poetics of parsimony, as an economics of generosity might be to our present economics of scarcity. For this search, Carolyn Kizer has been both moon and polar star, both illumination and guide.

The first I knew of Carolyn,[1] some time in the late 1960s, she was the author of a volume of poetry suffused with energy and marked by precision, delicacy, and strength of lyrical feeling. This was a poet who addressed a wide range of cultural contexts and associations and who was willing to tackle great and difficult subjects and to write unfashionable poems. At a time, for example, when the elegantly savage style of Augustan satire had maybe reached its nadir, this poet wrote "Pro Femina," which took the risk of talking about the condition of women long before that was an acceptable contemporary theme, and doing so in a style that for verve, wit, and polished outrage, not to say occasional venom, had not been heard since the satires of Pope. Both the lyricism and the wit, furthermore, struck me as those of a poet confident of her own powers and generous in her trust of her readers and of the poems themselves. This confidence made it unnecessary for her to hide behind either the careful construct of her irony or the pretense of a neuter voice, the first of which seemed obligatory for all poets who came of age in the 1950s and early 1960s, and the second obligatory for women writing at that time, as it had been for the generation that had preceded us.[2]

This forthrightly woman-centered voice and wholehearted commitment to the immediacy of the poem may have caused occasional misreadings of Carolyn's work. More often, however, reviewers made sensitive attempts to formulate accurate reactions to poems for which the feminist critical context and vocabulary either did not yet exist or were not yet widely understood. Hence one reviewer's courtly characterization of her as "Roman Matron and . . . Oriental Courtesan together."[3] Clearly it is possible, and even somewhat obvious, to read this as an unintentional put-down.[4] Such a reading fails to allow for the effect of characterizing an archetypal, a larger-than-life, a heroically mythic quality of the persona her poems construct. Yes, at times this persona speaks as matron, not simply as ordinary, everyday matron, but as legendary Matron, not housewife but incarnation of The Household, the archetypal character of Matron speaking with the weight of history and of generations of "the private lives of one-half of humanity."[5] At times she speaks as courtesan, not woman up for grabs but woman of erotic power and skill, who avowedly loves men, likes to court and please them, and who expects them to court and please her, too. At times she speaks as quintessential mother, as daughter, as wife (even somewhat balefully as ex-wife), and as friend. At times she speaks clearly and powerfully as citizen of the international community of poets, in the tone and with the authority of a poet who knows herself to have every right to first-class citizenship. And, in many of the poems, she speaks as Goddess, the role that can contain and engender all the other roles. This insistence on woman's centrality both in public and in personal contexts creates a vision of woman as herself a primary rather than a derivative incarnation of Blake's "human form divine," having, like Sir Thomas Browne, her own "peece of divinity in [her]."[6] Such a vision is central to the current feminist enterprise.

---

1. Since 1970 I have been a friend of Carolyn Kizer's. I am not going to create a false appearance of academic objectivity by referring to her by her surname. The value often placed on objectivity is counterproductive. Objectivity unmediated by personal involvement falsifies as much as unacknowledged or dishonest subjectivity. In any event, an involvement, a stake in something, whether or not it is acknowledged, always exists. One of my assets as a reader of Carolyn's poetry is precisely my lack of objectivity, my personal involvement, my immersion in her work. I suspect it would be hard to find a poet of her and my generation who had somehow managed to avoid knowing and having a personal involvement with her. Poets become friends much of the time because we feel affinities for each other's work. Those affinities lead to informed readings and then to close friendships.
2. On this subject, Juhasz in *Naked and Fiery Forms* is particularly useful. See her discussion of Marianne Moore, for example.
3. Richard Howard, in a review in *TriQuarterly*, reprinted on the dust jacket of *Midnight Was My Cry*.
4. Would this writer, or any, have characterized, for example, a poet like James Dickey as "Southern redneck and all-purpose stud?" If he had attempted such an irrelevancy, would he or Dickey's publisher have felt that the presence of such a comment on a book jacket might tend to sell books?
5. Carolyn Kizer, "Pro Femina: Part Three" in *Mermaids in the Basement* (Port Townsend, WA: Copper Canyon Press, 1986), 44.
6. William Blake, "The Divine Image"; Sir Thomas Browne, *Religio Medici*.

The Breath of Parted Lips: Voices from the Robert Frost Place, Volume I

FOREWORD

When Robert Frost was introduced as a farmer poet, he stuck out his hands, palms up: These aren't a farmer's hands, he would say. Famously, he declared that once a man had made a metaphor, it unfitted him for other work.

Frost had his chosen work, and we are thankful for it. He consecrated his whole life to the art of poetry.

When I met him, in August of 1945, he was seventy-one years old and I was sixteen. The first moment I saw him he was walking uphill toward an assembly room at Bread Loaf, and he seemed to rise from the ground like a stone figure. He was not stone, but he endured with the firmness of granite, obdurate in devotion to the art he loved. When I saw him in the last August of his life, he was deaf as granite, but spoke with his old skill, humor, and intensity. The books he was reading then rested beside his chair: Horace's Odes, and a new edition of Robinson's Chaucer.

He was not always an easy man. He was often an uneasy man, whatever fame and praise accrued to him. He cherished and defended his place among poets, and like Milton and Keats his ambition was boundless: He wanted above all to make poems that would last.

Unlike most of us, and many of the greatest poets, he mostly worked alone. If Frost worked little *with* other poets, he worked for poets and poetry. In 1957, in an introduction to an anthology of new poets, he wrote: "Young poetry is the breath of parted lips. For spirit to survive, the mouth must find how to firm and not to harden." To firm and not to harden. In Franconia's Frost Place, young poets learn to firm their mouths without hardening their hearts.

From its beginning in 1977, the Frost Place has celebrated ongoingness of American poetry. Every year, a younger poet spends the summer in Robert Frost's old house overlooking the glorious valley and the mountains beyond. The poet has a modest stipend, leisure, and the opportunity to work where Frost worked. Every year, the summer resident and other visiting poets read their poems aloud—summer performances of contemporary art among the

White Mountains. Visitors may walk where Frost walked and inspect the rooms where he lived with his family and wrote poems.

The Frost Place in Franconia is a monument to a great American poet. We need our monuments. We honor poetry as we honor the poet where the poet lived. Frost and his family resided in this Franconia house beginning in 1915 after they returned from England. Great poems were written in this house.

Poetry flourished at the Frost Place then and it flourishes there now.

Donald Hall
Eagle Pond Farm, New Hampshire

LAST THINGS

His children came as if their own good health could restore
his. He lost a little more each week, the tumor taking
his legs and then the memory of what just happened
moments ago. Still, he made not walking as matter-of-fact
as walking, found jokes in his forgetting. "Hello," he'd say,
picking up the phone, "You've just reached Bob's
Brain Tumor Clinic; leave a message and he may or may not
get back to you." How quickly he learned to help them again,
as if, as their father, there were these last things to do.
When pain flashed in his eyes, then drained away,
his children could see how their wanting him, even as he was,
would give them no peace. When he slept, they watched
him move inside his dream as if he were mapping
the circumference of everything he was taking leave of—
the newly planted weeping cherry just outside
the front door, the crocus and daffodils he forgot
the names of, and further off, the city he loved, bodiless
clouds skimming its horizon of buildings. Near the end,
papers came and went with the daily news, and faces,
each becoming another and another, flowing past him
like leaves on a childhood river. Half in delirium, he'd speak
of someone he couldn't see who kept coming for him.
Before he went, he waited for his children to come and say
goodbye. And when he was gone, they gathered
around him, and looked into his face, and touched the scar
on the back of his head where the tumor divided
the father they knew into bits and pieces. And each of them
found they had the strength to lift and hold his head
in their hands one last time, its weight the size of a world.

Grub, by Martin Mooney

THE GENERAL

Because today is Sunday and there is no war
to keep him at his desk, the General
has taken time off to come out in the sun.
Even so early the park is crowded
with men in shirt sleeves like himself:
his friend the Admiral sails a fleet
of paper battleships across the pond,
a Major of their acquaintance sags
in a deck chair near the bandstand, as
musicians from his regiment play
the themes from all his favorite movies,
The Dambusters, *A Bridge Too Far*. The General
finds himself whistling "Colonel Bogie"
as he strolls among the tanned civilians,
happy to let them lie there unconscripted,
all maps and strategies forgotten,
no coups and no conspiracies to plan.
He smiles, and the sun smiles back at him
from the glass towers of the financial district,
whose windows hold the image of a kite
that someone somewhere else is flying.

Apparition Hill, by Mary Ruefle

THE PEDANT'S DISCOURSE

Ladies, life is no dream; Gentlemen,
it's a brief folly: you wouldn't know
death's flashcard if you saw it.
First the factories close, then the mills,
then all of the sooty towns
shrivel up and fall off from the navel.
And how should I know, just because my gramma
died in one? I was four hundred miles away,
shopping. I bought a pair of black breasts
with elastic straps that slip over the shoulder.
I'm always afraid I might die at any moment.
That night I heard a man in a movie say
I have no memories and presumably he meant it.
But surely it was an act. I remember my gramma's
housedress was covered with roses. And she
remembered it too. How many times she turned
to her lap and saw the machines: the deep folds
of red shirts endlessly unfolding while they dried.
Whose flashcard is that? So, ladies and gentlemen,
the truth distorts the truth and we are in it up
to our eyebrows. I stand here before you tonight,
old and wise: cured of vain dreams, debauched,
wayward and haggard. The mind's a killjoy, if
I may say so myself, and the sun's a star,
the red dwarf of which will finally consume us.

Snakeskin Stilettos, by Moyra Donaldson

EXILE

What ground is mine
if I would govern myself?
Where is my country
if neither bogs nor gantries
speak of me?
Where can I stand
if I am not one thing
or the other?

My grandfather knew where he stood.
Ancestors planted his feet
in fertile soil, green futures were
named in his name, possessed.
He preached their flinty faith
in mission tents, visions of eternal life
on soft Ulster evenings,

but there was no redemption.
Not in the land, or through the Blood.
Not in the hard lessons of duty, obedience,
with which he marked his children.

He is stripped of virtue,
his legacy a stone
of no magic, no transcendence.
No children ever turn to swans,
wafer remains wafer on the tongue
and flesh is always flesh.

My two white birds will bring me
water from the mountains,

beakfuls of sweet sips.
I will grow a new tongue,
paint my body with circles
and symbols of strength, mark myself
as one who belongs in the desert.

Silk Elegy, by Sondra Gash

BREAD AND ROSES (MORRIS)

Paterson Police Chase and Club Strikers.
Bar Thousands From Meeting.
—*Paterson News*, February 1913

Every Sunday all through that winter
we gathered next door in Haledon—
23,000 strikers huddled for hours
on a field outside the home of a
weaver named Botto. John Reed,
Emma Goldman, and the Wobblies—
Bill Haywood, Gurley Flynn, Carlo
Tresca—stood on the balcony, shouting:

One big union. No more exploitation.
We want bread and we want roses!

The strike went on for months.
We were hungry and cold, our savings
gone. Some of us had to farm out
our children. The city's Cooperative
bakers donated loaves of pumpernickel
and seeded rye. Gifts poured in from
everywhere but the courts, the papers,
300 owners were all against us.

You're just workers. Morris. Give up.
There are no laws to protect you.
I didn't come here to be a slave, Lena.
If we stick together, we'll win.
String your big words on a line, they'll

just flap in the wind. She was right.
We lost and my boss Mr. Lambert
smiled down on us from his castle,
Bella Vista, 26 rooms on top of the hill.

The Palace of Ashes, by Sherry Fairchok

NEAR RATS AND THE DEVIL

The women of Taylor, Pennsylvania, watched from windows
while their men ran to the last blast of the company's whistle
and wouldn't step out until the great gates latched shut:
Bad luck for a man on his way to the mines to meet a woman.
In the dark, near rats and the devil, was the men's place.
No women went below.
                                        They worked under the sun's supervision,
flinging corn to geese, pinning up Monday laundry, burying bulbs
at the feet of plaster Virgins. No woman of Taylor ventured
any deeper than her cellar with its shelved jars shining in rows,
its slumbering crocks of pickles and sauerkraut, though their men
lugged down pails packed by women's hands with whatever simmered
on coal stoves the night before. That noon-hour whiff of kitchens tasted
of the brightness overhead, like the scent of wet lilacs trickling
down an air shaft in May.
                                        Rats ran to it, too, and ringed
each chewing man, their eye-glints red as lit cigarettes.
Stoned from alleys, poisoned in kitchens, chased by terriers
through backyards, rats were friends in the labyrinth
under the town. When the Susquehanna flooded tunnels,
men followed fleeing rats to dry ground and, ever after, sprang
with their picks all company-laid traps. When rats lingered
to gnaw at what was dropped, reared to beg crusts, miners knew
timbers propped overhead would hold. When rats ran,
you'd better run yourself home.
                                        Women were a different matter:
their bedrooms a tunnel a man entered in fear and wonder,
beneath a plastic crucifix but closer to the devil,
a dark space he worked at night, and crawled from
proud to have done his job, relieved to be out intact,
weak, trembling and homeless as an unearthed rat.

A Gradual Twilight: An Appreciation of John Haines, edited by Steven B. Rogers

FROM STORIES I HAVE LISTENED TO, BY STEVEN B. ROGERS

John Haines was born in Tidewater Virginia in 1924, and as the son of a career naval officer he frequently moved around the United States with his family. He never had an opportunity to put down real roots until 1947 following his own discharge from wartime naval service, when he and a friend set off to Alaska to find a patch of land to call their own. The friend quickly abandoned the adventure, but Haines settled at Richardson, on a hillside above the Tanana River almost 70 miles southeast of Fairbanks. Although he hoped to use the solitude at Richardson to focus on his art studies, he admits that his birth as a poet can be traced to his first real home, his homestead in Alaska: "I must have carried in myself from an early age some vague design of such a place and such a life. . . . From the first day I set foot in interior Alaska, and more specifically on Richardson Hill, I knew I was home. Something in me identified with that landscape. I had come, let's say, to the dream place" (*Living Off the Country*, 4–5). It was there that he began to write poetry seriously. In "The Hermitage," Haines writes:

In the forest below the stairs
I have a secret home,
my name is carved in the roots.

I own a crevice stuffed with moss
and a couch of lemming fur;
I sit and listen to the music
of water dripping on a distant stone,
or I sing to myself
of stealth and loneliness.

No one comes to see me,
but I hear outside

the scratching of claws,
the warm, inquisitive breath . . .

And once in a strange silence
I felt quite close
the beating of a human heart.

I have also learned to appreciate the precarious existence of a man and an artist whose very heart and soul are intrinsically tied to the Alaskan homestead where he lived and toiled and about which he has written so lovingly; a writer who has practiced his craft without the perks and comforts of university tenure, without a retirement plan, with little in the bank, who has made his living by his wits and words alone. Despite these hardships, John Haines continues to create poems and essays that capture the beauty of the natural world, to identify the threats to that way of life, and to offer wisdom as one who has patterned his life on the land that nurtured it.

> The physical domain of the country had its counterpart in me. The trails I made led outward into the hills and swamps, but they led inward also. And from the study of things underfoot, and from reading and thinking, came a kind of exploration, myself and the land. In time the two become one in my mind. With the gathering force of an essential thing realizing itself out of early ground, I faced in myself a passionate and tenacious longing—to put away thought forever, and all the trouble it brings, all but the nearest desire, direct and searching. To take the trail and not look back. Whether on foot, on snowshoes or by sled, into the summer hills and their late freezing shadows—a high blaze, a runner track in the snow would show where I had gone. Let the rest of mankind find me if it could. (*The Stars, the Snow, the Fire*, 19)

Works Referenced

Haines, John. *Living Off the Country: Essays on Poetry and Place*. Ann Arbor: The University of Michigan Press, 1981.

———. *The Stars, the Snow, the Fire*. St. Paul: Graywolf, 1989.

THE ALLIGATOR'S HUM

To allure an alligator lady so she'll allow him
To fertilize her eggs before she buries them
In her sand nest, the male alligator
Hums in a swamp pond like a kid in a bathtub.
It hums like a foghorn: *Hummmmmm!* And raises
Queer geysers of water by his torso's profound
Vibrations, these inverted, fragile, almost crystal
Chandeliers his obligatto of amor. I have tried this
On dates without knowing what I was doing:
Hummmmmm! My date pretended she didn't know
What I was doing either and would ask,
"Are you all right?" *Hummmmmm!* I'd echo,

Something below my solar plexus now governing
My lowest, reptilian, ganglion brain. But I swear,
Like people who claim they can't understand poetry,
She knew what it meant for the hum of the body
To dominate mind. It meant please admire
My wet inverted chandeliers, which translates,
Like all of poetry too, into alligator: *You can get me,*
If you let me, you grinning, beautiful,
Primordial swampwater creature you! Then their tails
Slap the water with a belly whomp.
They thrash like mad, almost invisible—though the human
Eye is never naked—and then it's over.

GlOrious, by Joan Cusack Handler

GRAVY

Forced to listen to the body's sentence
as it hesitates &faults, you learn to
trust its limitations.

Even love isn't enough.

Now even our coming together
in the first place gets questioned.

It's like that at Fifty.
I'm thinking again
about B i g things —
Happiness & Peace
— no longer vague,
they take on
a muscularity,
a defined
shape
like a chest or a back
that starts with a feeling
that t h i c k e n s
in the belly then Pushesup
into the biceps finally
collecting
at the bend
in the throat.
Life crystalizes
&we're not looking
so much for higher purpose but nuts & bolts:

I have it or I don't.

That's where we are now.
Our love I take for granted. Strange as it seems, it's gravy.

CHILD AND MOTHER

My tongue is small, it cannot weigh
the syllables I must obey.

These words will be your own in time;
they will forget that you were mine.

I know that I am yours when night
remembers, and I wake in fright.

Dear, fright is all we come to know;
when love's forgotten, fear must grow.

THE SOLID BODY

June spreads like butter.
I am a white smudge in its heat.
I know this melody and the crickets' music,
their back legs moving so fast.
I sometimes fall or fly
or am transported by tornadoes in my dreams.

I am ten, I am chubby, and I am running.
My feet and his pound over the hard red clay.
I jump the sty, into the blackberries,
in three long leaps. The briars and his belt lash me.
He is slower because of the drink.
He carries me through the long rows of pecan trees.
I lie so still after doing the daddy dance.

Soft Box, by Celia Bland

MATERNITY

Akhmatova writing odes to plows
to free her son—I know
that surrender now, that betrayal of self and art.
Those long waits outside
the prison gates, in snow.

It is terrible to love.
It was not the baby but the child repeating my
vowels, curses, verbs indiscriminately. Playing his toys
along my legs and stomach
as if I were only landscape.

PARTS OF SPEECH

for Bob Phillips

Don't bring me flowers, send me words
uncorked from thin-necked bottles
the wind spins in vertiginous waves.
Sometimes even a sigh will do
from the old dog heaving the three turns
it takes to make its bed; or the sheeps' swollen
stare from the pasture, their noisy tap dance
on the hollow trough, as they stumble
over a succulent call to supper.

Better than a string of pearls,
let me clasp those words;
so suave and blonde, they saunter
through the stands in polo coats
as smooth as sherry sipped from glasses
etched with hunters' whips and cornered beasts.

Not that I can't devour a bestial grunt
or groan, the brunt of stout four-letter
words, if that's what meets a human need.
But bring me words hammered out
from all the rest, faint at first, but grasped
alive, honking from an autumn sky, opening up
the line for me to climb; strong enough
to look straight into the starry sun—
and the speech I'm looking for.

The Breath of Parted Lips: Voices from the Robert Frost Place, Volume II

FROM DEMOCRACY, THE SPIRIT, AND POETIC PASSION

In a letter I received from him, the distinguished New Hampshire man of letters, Donald Hall writes: "Don Sheehan's disinterested passion for poetry, shaping the institution of the Frost Place, has made a monument exemplary in the purity of its attentions."

I've been involved with the world of American poetry for all my adult life. I have seen almost as much to chagrin me as I have to encourage. As poetry becomes less and less a vocation than a profession, as poets become members of a guild rather than practitioners of a sacred art, politics and networking too often prevail over more humane concerns.

Not at the Frost Place. Not under Don Sheehan's careful and caring stewardship. I can think of few if any undertakings that are as thoroughly democratic as the annual Frost Place Poetry Festival—or any of the Frost Place-sponsored events and programs that have come into being in its twenty-five years. It is this democratic urge that Don Hall has in mind, I think, when he speaks of "disinterested passion." Something very similar moves Maine Poet Laureate Baron Wormser, another longtime associate and supporter of the Frost Place, to suggest that "What has made the Frost Place so special for so many people is Donald Sheehan's vision, a vision that puts our capacity to care for one another at the center of the activities of the Frost Place."

Disinterest is, of course, a word often misconstrued to mean indifference, though what it really means is impartiality. The passion that makes the annual poetry festival at Franconia all but throb is impartial in the sense that it takes no heed of anyone's reputation, status, or influence. Important connections are made, to be sure, but they're made on the basis of the art itself and not of political or academic serviceability. They are, if I may use a tricky term, spiritual connections. Sheehan leads us all to understand that envy and competition are not only unwelcome at a Frost Place event but also, in the grander scheme, inimical to the very quality and survival of verse itself. Passion and care for one another as human beings not only can but also must coexist.

I am not Don Sheehan's spiritual peer. Few people are. Yet I have sought, however imperfectly, to assemble a book in his manner. I am above all pleased that persons whose poems have never been published appear here cheek by jowl with persons whose work has garnered the highest awards and distinctions available to American writers. I am particularly delighted by all the moving and deft poetry from writers whose names are at the moment unfamiliar to me and to most readers. Any decent editor will tell you that the surprise discovery is the truest reward he or she can savor. I have therefore been many, many times blessed by the scores of surprise discoveries I made in the process of editing this volume.

Once again, the greater credit goes to Donald Sheehan. No writers' gathering commands the fierce allegiance that the one in Franconia does. Participants and faculty members and resident poets alike testify to the Frost Place's benign impact on their craft. In letter after letter accompanying submissions to this book, the compound word *life-changing* appeared. I could desire nothing better than for the reader of *The Breath of Parted Lips, Volume II,* to feel his or her life likewise changed, however subtly, by its combinant poems. We often speak, though sometimes rather facilely, of poetry as "transformative"; if it reflects the spirit of Donald Sheehan and his programs, however, the poetry that follows will deserve that descriptive.

Sydney Lea
Newbury, VT
April 2004

"FOR MAY IS THE MONTH OF OUR MOTHER"

for Rosemary McLaughlin and Laurie Würm

When jump ropes smacked the softening tar
we took turns taking Mary home. She was white
with a blue screw-off bottom, supplicant hands,
and a rosary rattled inside as she swung in our book bags.
After supper is good for some, Sister Michael said,
or before bed. If you pray the rosary, Communism
will fall. When my turn alphabetically came for Mary,
I rattled her the two blocks up the hill,
but Catholic in our family was for kids, and Communism
was a word, not a stick or stone. My mother was tired,
my father was going to hell, I wasn't up to fifty Hail Mary's
alone, but I couldn't just dump Mary there on my cluttered dresser
like a glowing, white, wimpled bottle of shampoo
while I climbed the catalpa tree or played pies with the others,
so I set her down on our suitcase-shaped Victrola,
and put on Mom's Perry Como "Ave Maria."
Mary stood on her snake with her begging arms out, glowing.
The sky in the window grew orange, the breeze carried lilacs.
Next, I played Nelson Eddy, "Ave Maria." Her one-inch face
held too much sadness to bear. To cheer her up,
I played "Rum and Coca-Cola," the Andrews Sisters, and our souls
were so open from all that *ave maria* that we threw ourselves
into the rhythm, and jumped on the bed, and I beat Mary
like a maraca in my palm, her burden of black beads clacking
thick and loud, until one slap too many cracked her right in half,
and her beads flung themselves to the floor, where they lay
like intestines. I learned then to use something right
or leave it alone. No, I didn't. I learned *twelve-inch Virgin,*
polystyrene, luminous ivory, black beads in screw-off bottom

ran $4.95, or twenty weeks of allowance.
I learned too that Mary was real to crack like that,
and I saved a splinter of her shattered gown
and I know she is patron saint of the spring-cracked mind,
and mother of all who aspire to glow in the dark.

LAPS

In this marriage of water and air
always she is the beginner

teaching her hands and arms
to push away the water, to raise

her head, to breathe. Though
she swims her laps, butterflying

up and back, trying to kick loose
her leg muscles, the hamstrings

spasm, then left foot crosses right,
forces her to invent a one-legged

way to swim. No more can she
hoist her body out of the pool, or

climb the metal stairs. Instead
she sits in the hydraulic chair, waits

for someone to flick the switch.
Immobile in air,

gravity reclaims her.
In the locker room, there's

always a woman to pull up
her panties, stretch slacks, socks.

After years of early-bird swims
they know each other's bodies.

Wrinkling skin, diminishing limbs.
Nothing holds them back.

Life with Sam, by Elizabeth Hall Hutner

PRAYER

When I close my eyes, let me always
feel the ache under my breastbone
as it spreads down my belly to my legs,
out to my arms, to my fingers, my toes.
Let me remember my son just turned two,
hooked to a heart monitor, an IV
pumping medicine into his veins.
Let me let him go to surgery,
and let me let the machines take the place
of my arms. Let me watch the screens
instead of the rise and fall of his chest.
Let me be weak with sadness, let me cry
as I endure the separation.
I let him go, step by step, until he died.
I gave him the pills, I checked the blood counts,
I held his hand for the bone marrow tests.
I saw the little girl, healthy, who looked
away when she saw him, bald and dying,
in the X-ray room, but I have looked away
when the dying one was not my son.
Please let me also remember his voice
calling "Mom!" and his laugh as he ran to me
when I picked him up from preschool.
Let me feel the heaviness of his head
on my shoulder as he slept.
Even if it is only in memory,
let me hold his peaceful breathing
in my breath as the new baby grows
within me.

THE SINGERS I PREFER

The singers I prefer are the ones
who have to struggle. Famously,
there is Bob Dylan, and Robert Plant
who might have sung lower but
didn't. And now there is this
Beth Orton who seems to be singing
through a wall. Through a wall?
I would really like to get this
right. Granted, the perfect voices
on the radio today singing the "Ode to Joy"
made me cry but I was thinking—
in between the floating, the deep
hunger of dream-memories—of deaf
Beethoven locked in his smelly room,
Beethoven who probably never had
a woman groan his name in the clutch,
scribbling each note at an audience
of clefs and inkwells. It was after her face
had been scarred in the accident, when
her mouth would only open on one
side, when it tasted of acrid medicines
and something deathlike
that I saw for the first time how
beautiful M was, how damn
funny. If not through a wall, then
through some almost crippling pain,
the kind that threatens to blot out
all the sweetness, even the bursting through
of a hundred ecstatic voices
in a pickup truck in Bangor, Maine
in a snowstorm, after a long sadness.

WHEN YOU TELL ME

When you tell me I
should keep the house
and furniture, the air
inside the car is like
the breath a woman holds,
breaking eggs against
a bowl or listening
for the sound of shoes
in the bedroom, the closet
door closing where her
husband has just
stood, choosing a tie.

YOUR DREAM

A big dog is digging up a hole.
In it lie seven or eight dead puppies.
"My dead babies," you say and wake up.

This morning when you tell me your dream
I cry. "I'm sorry I told you," you repeat,
but I'm not. For the first time, I feel

your grief. Hours later, still in my robe,
I wander to the window. It hardly seems
possible there are people out there going

about their business. The sky is ridged
with the kind of clouds that bring snow.
On the sill, jars full of rocks from

every stream you fished or we hiked
the summer we lived in the shadow
of the Divide. My shaking hands find

the chunk weathered out of the earth
at Animas Forks. Pale as the overcast
heavens that changeable day, its rough

edges smoothed by eons of water rushing
to the sea and as cold as the snowmelt
feeding the stream, I lift it up to

my flushed cheek, hoping it will cool
a too swift heart that wants to burst.

Common Life, by Robert Cording

THE WEEPER

The name his followers gave Ignatius, who wept
While saying mass, or while listening to the coos
Of a common dove. Ignatius never knew
When his throat would tighten, a wave of sobs
Breaking him open as he stood watching clouds
Move in the wide gaze of the sky, or passed a boy
Climbing a pine, lost in the play of his body.
Yet it wasn't the reverie of blue sky and clouds,
Nor even the boy's self-forgetful happiness
That brought on those tears beyond his control.
These days, when passion is cooled by irony,
When we try to live as if each day were
Predictable and self determined, when God
And the soul are off-limits, how can we understand
Such abandonment in a man who wept
Almost daily—not because of the time he'd wasted
Or would waste, not because of his weak stomach
Or his leg's old war injury, or because he'd given up
The feel of trembling flesh along the inner curve
Of a woman's thigh or the full, idle hours
Spent in his father's castle. Not even because of
The wearied and hopeless poor whom he met
On every road and went among in cities.
He wept, they say, because he'd suddenly feel
Entirely empty, and utterly grateful, all the doors
Of his heart, which was and was not his
At these moments, and which we know
Only as metaphor, swung wide open, able now
To receive and find room for all the world's
Orphaned outpourings and astonishments.

AFTER DROUGHT

Knees rooted in the bed on either side
of your belly, my body's a stalk of wheat
bent in summer wind, a bamboo shoot
rising, an orchid, and then all at once a cloud
swelling, a swallow sculpting air, a freed
white dove. You pull me down, but you are hot
beneath me, and the gust that is my own heat
lifts me away: I'm not ready. Outside,
footsteps, voices. Two men. Giggling, we pull
the sheet around us till they pass, but if someone
does see, what will they have seen? A couple
making love. No. More than that: They will
have seen the coming of the rain; they will
have seen us bathe in it, and they will say *Amen*.

NEW YEAR'S EVE

I go out on New Year's Eve. I hate New Year's Eve but it's the year 2000 and so I have to go out and have fun so I go to my friend Linda's house and Linda serves a good meal, tarts and roasts and rack of lamb and Linda's sister Pattie brings wine and the wine is equal to the meal. Light, airy whites, thick, rich reds, and finally a dessert wine, a German wine, slick and sugary and this isn't a bad way to come to the next century, I think, but there's more to do. I'm invited to another party to ring in the new, so I say goodbye and everyone's mad at me, no surprise there, and I go to Danny and Caroline's for music and drink. Danny and Caroline's is filled with children. Children and parents of children and there is music but there is also parents yelling at children and children saying please, please, please. But there is also wine and I'm happy for that and there is talk with good friends and that's not bad and there's this guy holding forth and smoking tons of cigarettes and Caroline says that's my friend Mike Latch and we talk for a good while and this guy is wired up like some junior Neal Cassady and we're drinking red wine from Bulgaria, bulls blood, and the cigarettes are everywhere. Then he reads Rimbaud for the millennium, then there are fireworks everywhere and the sky is filled with red and white and green flowers and it's officially the next day, next month, next year, next century and I feel good that I didn't do anything wrong for once but just eat and drink and talk with my friends on a night not so strange, except for red filling the sky.

Against Which, by Ross Gay

PULLED OVER IN SHORT HILLS, NJ, 8:00 A.M.

It's the shivering. When rage grows
hot as an army of red ants and forces
the mind to quiet the body, the quakes
emerge, sometimes just the knees,
but, at worst, through the hips, chest, neck,
until, like a virus, slipping inside the lungs
and pulse, every ounce of strength tapped
to squeeze words from my taut lips,
his eyes scanning my car's insides, my eyes,
my license, and as I answer the questions
3, 4, 5 times, my jaw tight as a vice,
his hand massaging the gun butt, I
imagine things I don't want to
and inside beg this to end
before the shiver catches my
hands, and he sees,
and something happens.

From *To the Marrow*, by Robert Seder

I'm still getting used to this place. This is my home. I can't tell you I'm claustrophobic or that I hate the place or this is even the last place in the world you'd want to be. There are worse places. You don't want to be in Bosnia, although you could survive that war and have no cancer. You don't want to be on death row. You don't want to be living on the street, not in January in Boston. But you don't want to be here. We put up photos of the kids. And some of Clare's drawings. I brought a few books, but have barely looked at them. I brought paper and pencils, but the tape recorder is all I can manage right now. I've asked friends to send snapshots of themselves instead of cards. They think I'm strange—But hey, whatever you want; better you than me. You don't want to be here. The photos and drawings don't make me cry anymore. They've become wallpaper. All these people on the outside going about their business. Me in here. Pisses me off. Jean's been the only visitor so far. They call. They complain about the weather. It snows. It's cold. They tell me I picked a good time to be indoors for a month. They tell me I'm better off inside. Bull. I am not well off. Or am I? In a good hospital with people who know what they are doing and care. I couldn't be better. I have something my callers don't. I have a chance today and tomorrow and for the next however long it takes to fight the thing that could kill me.

When I talked about death, people would respond with some version of—Any of us crossing the street could be hit by a bus. I'd respond—Yeah, but when I get to the other side of the street I will still have cancer. What I'm doing here is trying to let the bus hit the cancer, but to jump my self out of the way at the last second. Jump too soon and the cancer jumps with me. Jump too late . . .

Later they will come and take me back to the radiation chamber for my second dose and do the whole thing over again. They have to split up my dosage into six sessions over three days. One humongous dose would be too much for me all at once. Jump.

THE EDGE

They had traveled a long way,
each from a beginning the others
couldn't imagine. When they
reached the edge, they all peered
deeply, as far as they could.

Almost at once, they gasped
and held onto each other. Then,
one declared, "I knew it. Beyond,
there is nothing." Another countered,
"For me, it holds everything." By now,
the fearful one fretted, "I knew I should
never have come." Dizzied by the view,
he retreated, "I must go back."

Finally, the blind one poked his way
to the edge and after a while sighed,
"It's as I've always known."

It was too late to travel down and so
they were forced to listen to each other
through the night.

The blind one began, "What will you
bring back?" The one who saw nothing
said, "That where we are is all there
is. That's what I'll say."

The one who saw everything smiled,
"I'll bear witness that we are cradled
by something incomprehensible."

At this, the fearful one jumped in,
"Well, my advice will be
to just stay put."

In the silence that followed,
they asked the blind one who
confessed, "I'm not going back."

THE MAN WHO COULD NOT TALK ABOUT THE WAR

He grabs her arm, seizing her from sleep
at three a.m. *Don't Move.*
There's someone here. Next to us.
She looks into the darkness
then again to his face, filled now
with transparency, carried back
to the jungle, to the ambush.
Her eyes search the vacancy
of moonlight on the window.
It's a dream she tells him.
We're all right. Go back to sleep.

He sinks back to silent breathing
until suddenly he flings his arm
across her shoulder. *Stay where you are*, he shouts.
This place is full of mines.
Help them, help them but she cannot
see the bodies or hear the sounds they make.

She lies in the narrowness
of one side of the bed,
touching his hand until light
seeps through the window across the contour
of the no one who is there.
Waking, he reaches for her
and turning to him she thinks
of the things that can be shared:
a table, a bed.

Imago, by Joseph O. Legaspi

IMAGO

As soon as we became men
my brother and I wore skirts.
We pinched our skirt-fronts into tents
for our newly circumcised penises, the incisions
prone to stick painfully to our clothing.

I was partial to my sister's plaid skirt,
a school uniform she outgrew; my brother favored
one belonging to my grandmother, flowers
showering down his ankles.
By this stage, the skin around the tips
of our penises was swollen the size
of dwarf tomatoes.

As a cure, my mother boiled
young offshoots of guava leaves.
Behind the streamline of hung fabric,
I sat on a stool and spread
before a tin washbasin. My mother bathed
my penis with the warm broth,
the water trickling into the basin like soft rain on our roof.
She cradled my organ, dried it with cotton,
wiping off the scabs melted by the warmth,
and she wrapped it in gauze, a cocoon
around my caterpillar sex.

I then thought of the others at the verge of their manhood:
my brother to replace me on this stool,
a neighborhood of eleven-, twelve-, and thirteen-year-old
boys wearing the skirts of their sisters
and grandmothers, touched

by the hands of their mothers,
baptized by green waters,
and how by week's end
we will shed our billowy skirts,
like monarchs, and enter
the gardens of our lives.

We Aren't Who We Are and this world isn't either, by Christine Korfhage

PICTURE PERFECT

In those days, after putting the baby
down for a nap, I'd tidy up.
And when there was no toy out of place,
no dish unwashed, no speck of dust
on the white kitchen counter or floor,
no smudge on the piano, no fingerprints
on the windows, glass-topped tables,
or patio doors, I'd stare at the phone.
Sometimes I'd open the drawer under it,
take out the Yellow Pages,
and look up "psychiatrist."
Once or twice I started to dial.
But the thought of exposing
so much disarray would send me
outdoors, past tubs filled with jasmine
to the lounge chair by the pool overlooking
the dock with the gleaming white boat
tied up to it. And whoever happened
to sail by, notice the scent of jasmine,
and glance up, would see me sitting there,
tanned and pretty in my straw hat
and bikini, sipping iced tea with ice cubes
made of lemonade and springs of mint,
looking perfectly happy.

Elegy for the Floater, by Teresa Carson

AUTOPSY REPORT

A possible ID in the pocket
which is wet and dirty and undecipherable
at this time.

The chain had been padlocked
around the neck and waist and chest regions,
however, hands and feet were free.

The body was placed in a wastebasket.
The cinder blocks were freed
after cutting the chain. Keys found
in the pocket fit the locks.

The Doctor also stated the deceased was
distraught after the death of his mother
who died 2-18-86.

In shirt pocket: prescription for
#1 Prolixin Hydrochloride
#2 Inderal
#3 Cogentin
#4 (scored out)
#5 Chloral Hydrate

The socks are well worn.
The shoes have holes in the heels.
Located within the two thighs and from inside
the underwear is removed dead fish.
Earlobes are partially eaten off.

No identifying scars, tattoos, or deformities
noted at this point in time.

December 1985: While driving on
Bergen Ave. I saw him—head bent
against the cold—but didn't stop.

He worshipped Houdini and retold
the stories of his most famous feats.
Especially, the Chinese Water Torture Cell.

When I visited him at Meadowview
he ignored the shouting patient,
who paced close to where we sat,
and said: Don't come here again.

He slept in Mom's bed after she died.

At her wake he sat in a corner
dressed in clean burgundy corduroy
pants and a flannel shirt that was
baggy in his near-skeletal frame.
He held his arms down but couldn't
stop the Prolixin-caused shakes.

When I told him how no one
in the family liked my house because
it was plain, he said: I like it;
it's a classic wood-frame
working-class house.

He taught me to make kites from
rice paper, balsa, electric blue paint.

Set of inked prints of recovered body (John Doe).
Note: due to decomp there is no better set avail,
however fingers are available. (Exhibit A)

What do I have to remember him
by? Two books he gave me (Keats,
The Bestiary), one black&white
photo—a profile shot.

Above subject (victim) is a mental patient.

The nurse at Medical Center:
Miss, your brother cannot have matches.

THE BOOK OF CRIME

Cooped-up men in jail
for sin or worse, I have turned
away from their words.

In my own cell now,
picturing wind keeps me
from sleep. How much
I would barter for one single breeze.

The Poetry Life: Ten Stories, by Baron Wormser

FROM GREGORY CORSO, B. 1930

Like the kids I work with, Gregory Corso was a runaway. He didn't have a home to speak of; his mom, who was sixteen when she had him, went back to Italy and left him in New York City. He wound up in orphanages and foster homes. When his father remarried and took him in, he still kept running away. He got in trouble—petty theft. A kid named Amos once told me that stealing was the way to go: you get caught swiping a pair of jeans and get sent to the county jail where you are entitled to a bed, warm meals, and a roof over your head. It beat sleeping under a highway overpass.

There aren't many days when at some random moment—I'm filling out a referral form for services or reading a memo or regaling my otherwise empty automobile with lines from a favorite poem—I don't remember a particular kid and wonder what happened. The kid in this case—Amos—was an optimist, a born hustler always trying to turn a dime into a quarter. In the old days he would have been doing card tricks on the sidewalk and separating the credulous from their money. Where in the "dire miasma" (to quote Gregory) is Amos? He exited through a window of our so-called "haven" in the middle of the night—a runaway from the runaways.

Gregory Corso did some serious time—three years—beginning when he was seventeen. That's not very old to do time. He was brutalized in prison. Anyone who's thought twice about what happens in prisons knows what that means. He read a lot of books, too. He discovered the freedom of poetry while in jail. I want to write, "How ironic is that?" but I'm not sure about irony. There are too many strange corners where you can't tell the shadows from the lights. Irony is too easy. Gregory said about his jail time, "I left there [prison] a young man, educated in the ways of men at their worst and at their best. Sometimes, hell is a good place—if it proves to one that because it exists, so must its opposite, heaven exist." I have that quote on the door of my tiny office.

ELEGY

My father knew we were afraid and he was also afraid so that night after dinner, he brought a chair from the kitchen, put a shotgun across his lap and rocked back and forth & was cold because the sun went down early and the blackness of the woods around us made the world seem still and I felt like a young boy that everything was going to last forever because my father was outside our house ready to fight to protect myself, my mother, and younger brother. I have wondered why I have not heard much about men like my father instead of those songs that sing why do you treat me so . . . my father was not a good man seldom home and mean to my mother and short-tempered with his sons. But he was that night the father I remembered sitting on the porch because he heard a Negro had talked back to some white man in town.

HANDS

In the dark before surgery hands dance over me beckon me all around me hands green hands hands smeared with blood fingers like elongated legs find silent pockets hide things there take them away outside the sun cuts the ice on the Hudson and I struggle like those ice fists the current so hot rushing beneath "Keep your hands off me!" I scream (should have/wished I screamed) when the subway stranger shoves his fingers between my thighs so many people cannot see his mouth jeering behind me I tighten my thighs and vaginal lips try to inch away but he pushes further I must change the way I dress see how quick we are to blame ourselves and where do I go from black shirtwaist and blazer Blue hands green hands mottled red and white hands Christ's hammered palms the beggar's ancient palms In some far off city two men send huge cupped palms to grab my breasts broad daylight no gasp or scream no one looks business as usual least of all me what most astounds me is my silence the huge breath sucked into my chest stuck there gagging me leaving me voiceless the merry-go-round not stopping no one stopping shouting this is his privilege what is it that tells one man the world is his we're all out there as banquet what makes one take the other let him like those chocolates bitten into then returned teeth arcs and all to their little cups in their heart shaped box and speaking of teeth marks I never noticed the surgeon's fingers how could I have missed them All five doctors questioned researched diplomas voices ages manners scrutinized but I can't remember the hands the fingers the length of the fingers the palms and thumbs are they smoke-stained nails framed with oil and blood do they tremble when he gets anxious my son and I stop everything to tear at our cuticles when we get scared

MY MOTHER WAS MEDEA

An absurd delusion, perhaps, but
I maintain she always loved me
even as her dagger pierced my chest
and I felt my breath go black and tight.
There was much aggravation beforehand
and I had never been the easiest child.
Plus, you should understand
her own childhood had left scars.
Certainly, my father was always difficult
and stirred up trouble whenever he was around.
I knew how things had to turn out
I was young, yes, but I knew:
early on I had presentiments of my end
and I felt pangs for my poor mother
when I realized she would be its instrument.
I do not forgive her. Don't get me wrong:
there is nothing to forgive. Love
may mean murder more often than we know
and as soon as I understood this I lost all fear.
Even so, I admit I was not wholly brave:
I flinched when she approached,
her eyes full of such terrible love.
But I was not altogether an innocent victim—
I knew my death was necessary
to punish my father, and when the moment
arrived I stood forth and waited.
When the blade struck bone
my hand guided *her* hand.

CANT / DESCANT

He's been taken to doctors and he's been taken to priests,
and he's been studied by all breeds of physicians and prophets.

They've promised this and promised that but haven't promised a cure. Still,
there's always a follow-up appointment to keep.

"Bring the boy back next week."

Shall I admire their relentlessness and optimism?

"Bring the boy back next week."

Why?

What is he? *A guinea pig?*

Fuck you.

Fuck you and fuck the sham shamans who blame it on the devil.
Fuck them, and fuck the devil: I will in my rage
possess him and fuck him.
And forget not the quacks in their white aprons, fucking con artists.
Fuck their reams of empirical data and their clinical observations.
Fuck their med school degrees, their bank accounts, and their investments.
Fuck charts.
Fuck prescriptions and drugs, fuck reports of medical
breakthroughs.
Fuck MRIs. Fuck X-rays.
And the psychiatrists and the psychologists:
fuck their fancy analysis, because
none of this drivel lights up my brother's eyes
like his mother's kiss.

ANNE FRANK EXHIBIT

a sign above the bed instructs us to imagine sleeping
here without name without detail's thread without
weight the stairway's one direction waking soundless
shoulder to shoulder looking through the curtain's hole
sized for watching the street where people are talking
are holding things crossing the river's blue gray water
whose banks are green are bare of wind carrying
rain or snow against glass lifting dust to a windowsill
a fingerprint in the next room my husband and I hear
the murmur of voices an automobile a piano chord
the book pulled from a shelf & pages falling open *rain*
snow falling on a field dug open burned open soil &
root the word *breath* breath without transfer held here

Losing Season, by Jack Ridl

AT FIFTY

Coach hurls the ball against the garage door,
grabs it on the rebound. He's missed ten
in a row. He steps to the line, bounces
the ball twice, hard, and the fans from
thirty years ago send their hopes across
their weary lungs. He listens to the hush
of the home crowd while the taunts
of those from out of town float through
the rafters down across the backboard,
spinning around and around the rim.
He slams the ball one more time, feels
the leather, eyes the hoop, shoots.
The ball caroms off the back of the rim, rolls
across the driveway into the herb garden
his wife planted the year they found this house.
Once he could drop nine out of ten
from the line, hit half his jump shots
from twenty feet. Coach sits down at
the top of the key, stares, sees himself
bringing it up against the press, faking,
shaking his shoulders, stutter stepping, shifting
the ball left hand to right, then back, then up,
his legs exploding, his wrist firing, the ball
looping up, down, through the hoop, making
the net shimmer, the crowd roar. He gets up,
goes over to the garden, reaches for the ball,
stops, and pulls some weeds growing through
the oregano, basil, sage, and thyme.

Southern Comfort, by Nin Andrews

BATHING IN YOUR BROTHER'S BATHWATER

Bathing, Miss De Angelo informed us in health class,
is very important, especially once you become a teenager.
In fact I can smell many of you this very day,
so I advise every one of you girls
to go home and take a good long bath tonight.
I know some of your folks like to skimp on water,
but consider it homework.
Say Miss De Angelo assigned it to you.
But girls, let me warn you.
Never take a bath in the same water as your teenage brother.
Why?
Well picture this.
All those tiny bubbles settling on your legs
when you sit in a nice tub of water?
If you could count every itty, bitty bubble,
that would be only a fraction of how many sperm
stream from a single man.
Even if he doesn't touch himself,
the water does.
And it only takes one.
One fast-moving whip-tailed sperm.
And you know how easy it is to catch a cold,
how quickly that little virus races clear through you.
And once that happens,
no one will believe you're any Virgin Mary,
no matter what you say.

Underlife, by January Gill O'Neil

EARLY MEMORY

I remember picking up a fistful
of sand, smooth crystals, like hourglass sand
and throwing it into the eyes of a boy. Johnny
or Danny or Kevin—*he* was not important.
I was five and I knew he would cry.

I remember everything about it—
the sandbox in the corner of the room
at Cinderella Day Care; Ms. Lee,
who ran over after the boy wailed for his mother,
her stern look as the words *No snack* formed on her lips.
My hands with their gritty, half-mooned fingernails
I hid in the pockets of my blue and white dress.
How she found them and uncurled small sandy fists.

There must have been such rage in me, to give such pain
to another person. This afternoon,
I saw a man pull a gold chain off the neck
of a woman as she crossed the street.
She cried out with a sound that bleached me.
I walked on, unable to help,
knowing that fire in childhood
clenched deep in my pockets all the way home.

WAITING

We wait for babies to be born, for test results to come back, for phone calls, jobs; we wait beside beds where people lay dying; we wait for love. Today I am waiting on the top of a mountain for the sun to rise. I shiver as wind bites through the crowd huddled together looking east. An old monk chanting prayers reminds me of the ancient people who once called the great sun to come back from where it hides in the night.

I can barely see the barren landscape around me, barely remember how I got here. There was the waking knock on the door at two a.m. I slipped on my clothes, filled my jacket pockets with what might be needed for the climb, then joined the others of our group on the monastery's guest house terrace. We set off, giving ourselves to the big bowl of darkness, to the stars and the small path shone by the light of our own flashlights.

As we pass through the monastery gates we're almost at once in the river of other travelers. The trail of hikers and camels zigzags a winding way up the mountain. The walk is long. The night is spectacular. We stop to rest, lean against the ancient rock and look into the enormous sky face. All the constellations I know and many I don't know; the swath of galaxies. Sometimes strings of 7 or 8 camels take up almost the whole path and force us to the side, kicking dust in our faces. My body aches. It's completely dark except for the brightest stars I've ever seen. We keep walking. An hour. Another hour. And another.

Now the steepest, rocky way to the summit. Over 1500 so-called steps from this point—just uneven pieces of stone, like a path of repentance, you just keep going, unable to look up or down, just one foot after the other, breathing—you and the mountain and the breath. This is waiting in motion. How much farther? Voices whisper "five more minutes, ten more minutes, we're almost there" to no one in particular. My legs are too tired to go on but I go on. I hear murmurs, a kind of quiet buzz, and feel a sudden wind. We're here.

The morning star rising and the silver sliver of moon setting, rose light across the mountaintops layering out into the distance as far as I can see. The slowly spreading gift of light. Waiting. Waiting. When the first arc of sun crosses the horizon, some people break into song—Greek? Arabic? Hebrew?—words I don't understand but the melody feels completely familiar. The red sun rises, the ritual spreading back and forth across time, ah, the moment when the world transforms from dark to light. We are always waiting in the circle of changes. And the world is never totally in darkness.

Susan Jackson
Mount Sinai

Descent, by John Haines

FROM READINGS FROM AN ALASKAN JOURNAL

Why write? Why tell stories and construct poems? Why labor over words and their meanings? Why struggle with thoughts, and with those elusive feelings, like fish falling through a net too large? Self-expression, in the most obvious and playful sense of this? Or is it something a few of us learn to do, and which happens to attract some attention in the world at large and, if we are lucky, may provide a living? It may be a little of all of these, but I think the most genuine justification for writing, for creating what we call literature, lies in this: that we are always, as writers and as individuals, under the obligation to give some account of ourselves and the world we have known, and that this activity remains one of the few ways we have of continuing ourselves in some truth and life in common.

Wendell Berry wrote something once I would like to quote: "we are dependent for understanding, and for consolation and hope upon what we learn of ourselves from songs and stories. This has always been so, and it will not change."

It is, in other words, a serious matter, and not to be taken lightly. I have always tried to approach my own life experience with some sense of this responsibility. It has not been easy. I have nonetheless been trying all my life to understand the ground I walk on, and as a writer to tell as well as I can what I have found, what I think I know. All I have is this one imperfect and unfinished life, with the things, events, and persons that have in one way or another found a place in it, and who therefore have some claim upon it. I must do my best by them, believing that if what I have seen and felt has any truth in it, that truth, or sense of life, will have meaning for others.

I like the old things and ways; the older I get, the better I like them. We hear it said of someone that he or she is "living in the past." This is taken to be a negative comment whenever applied. Personally, I see nothing wrong with living in the past; it is a perfectly good place to live. At the same time, I have to say that the demarcation seems to me to be false. It may be that only among such a perpetually transient and unsettled people as we North Americans have become that this division of life into past, present, and future could have become so accepted and pernicious in our thinking.

I believe it has not always been this way. In my mind, it ought not to be. The *right* place to live is a place in which past and present flow as a single experience, and together they make up the only future we are likely to have, the only sane and decent one.

Perhaps what all of this comes down to is *residence*, in the truest and deepest sense. What does it mean to be here? What clues can we find in the soil around us to the life that has been, is now, and may be tomorrow? Here in Alaska, as well as elsewhere, we can see how difficult is that needed residence, and the harm that continual change and uprooting inflicts on a land and its people. I know it all too well myself. Having lived and worked in many other places in recent years, I find myself drawn back in one way or another to the only ground I really know, in a kind of gentle bondage.

So I return to that obligation I spoke of at the beginning. For me, the writing is another phase of the life lived. Properly speaking, there would be no discontinuity, but ideally and at last, a reconciliation.

And finally, as for the significance of all this, perhaps it is a little like something an old, blind Irish storyteller once said to a woman tourist who asked him the age of some weathered and ciphered stones by the roadside in rural Ireland. And he replied: "Madam, we are much too young to know."

Letters from a Distant Shore, by Marie Lawson Fiala

FROM MIRROR, MIRROR

"Mom, do you have a mirror?" Jeremy asked, lying flat on his back in his hospital bed.

"Why, sweetie?"

"I want to see what I look like."

I felt first surprise, then a sharp stab of realization. *Of course, he's been lying in bed for a month while things were being done to him. He has no idea what he looks like after all that.*

I coaxed him into a few days' delay. "Jeremy, your hair needs cutting," I said. "The front is short and the back is long. Let's wait until I can find a pair of electric hair clippers and even out your haircut."

"Oh, okay. I always wanted a buzz cut." He smiled and agreed easily, in no hurry to face himself.

—

Jeremy's eyes were old, older than he was, older than anyone's who had not seen his own death close at hand. One sees the same look in photographs of people who have felt great cruelties. "I have suffered much," Jeremy's eyes said, "and I will suffer more, and still, I go on."

"Jeremy, dear, you know that you've been very sick. I don't want you to be surprised. You look different from how you used to look, okay? When you get better, you'll look like yourself again."

But still he said, "Mom, I want to see," and I gave the mirror to him.

Jeremy stared at his image for a long time. His lips quivered and tears ran down his face. "Mom, I look so awful," he said finally. "I didn't know I had scars. The scars look so bad." His lips pressed together hard and formed an upside-down *U*. He gave one deep sob, and then he put the mirror down and was quiet.

"Sweetie, you don't look awful; you just look sick. Soon you'll get better, your hair will grow out and cover the scars, and you'll look just like you did before, sweetie. Please don't be sad."

Jeremy looked up at me with a steady gaze and nodded once or twice but did not speak, then turned his face away and closed his eyes.

The mirror hadn't lied. I had. I knew that it was a lie even as I said the words, and Jeremy probably knew it too. No matter how much rehabilitation he underwent, Jeremy would not look the same. He would not *be* the same. The damage had been too great. From now on, for the rest of his life, he would always be a broken bird, too injured to fly freely.

How the Crimes Happened, by Dawn Potter

HEAVY METAL

With what care you compromise your righteous taste
for noise in service to your rampant sons;
linger like a pirate over Goodwill bins, the waste
of wretched yard sales, sifting one by one

the halt, the lame; then slip into the kitchen
after dark, kiss my shoulder, unload groceries,
pour a second beer, and, offhand, think to mention
you've just purchased our first-ever AC/DC

record. You!—dear secret and embarrassed owner
of Boston, Wings, and K-Tel disco albums,
derider of Pete Seeger and the Weavers, stalwart hater
of the Beach Boys, despiser of dull stoner jams—

you closet Modern Lover, not forgetting that a young
boy needs to shake his ravished parents all night long.

Divina Is Divina, by Jack Wiler

DIVINA IS DIVINA

My beloved had a friend.
My beloved is Johanna.
Her friend is Divina.
Of course, my beloved's real name is Marko
and her friend's real name is Hector.

My beloved brought Divina to my home.
She spoke no English.
I spoke no Spanish.
Of course I spoke a little Spanish and
Divina tried a little English.

My beloved and I have two dogs.
Divina loved our dogs and took them out.
When she came to visit she would stand outside
and cry, Johanna, and inside the dogs would cry.

My beloved's friend Divina died.
Not suddenly. Not prettily, not like anyone should die.
She died in a hospital in the city of New York
and no one knew her name.

She was Hector Gomez.
She had no family.
She lay quiet and still and faded into the world.
No one in the hospital knew Divina.

If we had stood outside and shouted her name
they would have walked us to the side
and asked us to leave.

They wouldn't have been jumping up with joy to hear our cry
like my dogs, like Johanna, like me.

So my beloved's friend met her end alone.
In a city hospital.
With no dogs prancing around her.
No flowers blooming.
Even though it was spring.

You could say, and you should,
what the fuck is this?
You could be angry, and you should.
What kind of world tosses humans in the trash?

But that would be like asking why the leaves
blow in the fall.
It would be like asking why flowers wilt in hot sun.
It would be like asking why Hector is Divina.

Hector is Divina because the flowers bloom!
Hector is Divina because the sun rises!
Hector is Divina because she is.
Because we are.
Because the sun is.
Because we die.
Because.
Because.
Hector is Divina because we need to hear
someone outside our door crying our names.
Divina is Divina.

WITHOUT END

Because she gave him life, she must bury
her dead child inside herself,
a labor without end, but one she undertakes.
Because she gave him life once,
she must do so again, one cell at a time if necessary:

limb buds, pits where his blue eyes will be,
caverns and ridges to reveal a brain
and heart, his neck and face;
and after, those first signs of wrists and ankles,
his five webbed fingers and toes.

Her child will not toss or turn or kick for more
space as he once did. He will not be reborn.
She knows this. But because she gave him life,
her child must be carried with her—there is no other way—
for the full term of her remaining life.

18

When I look back at the girl I was, she is as distant as a heron
    at the end of the marsh,
but each year the fog about her grows thinner & thinner—
    the fog of stupidity & prejudice—
& of the sorrow I feel for my mother who feared scorn,
    whose buried dreams
wracked her body, for my father's belief no decent man
    would ever have me. What were
the moonscape scratchings of that girl's nature that had
    her keep the child despite
each voice's admonition? How did she school herself into
    a generous life? I'd like to think
she saw a pattern beyond the evident confusion, but that
    wasn't so. She was lost & at risk,
probably delusional. Still she lived, the child I was who
    bore a child, as if she knew that if only
she'd grow light enough, there was someplace I'd finally
    carry her.

Impenitent Notes, by Baron Wormser

TRAVEL

The train swayed past cropped fields,
Barking collies, abandoned gas works, cows,
Brown bungalows with little gardens
And potting sheds, kids kicking a soccer ball
Down a deserted street. Behind me two teenage girls
Dressed in identical vests and white blouses talked.
"I hate people who are good," one of them said.
"They want you to be good too." "I know," the other one said.
"My Aunt Mary is like that. She makes me retch."
I rose and walked down the wobbling aisle toward
The space between cars. Two guys were sharing a pint
In the boyish, conspiratorial way men do.
I stretched my short legs and smiled at their whiskey.

Night creeping over the western hills, the lights of
The villages along ridges. I wanted to stride into
A house and be welcomed like a long-lost uncle.
I wanted to see everyone rise excitedly.
I wanted to smell the cooking, the wash, the closets,
The cats, the honest odors of bustling flesh.
I wanted to hug muslin, wool, linen.

The girls kept talking but in lower and tenser voices.
Two more stops to the terminus, a tiny station
From where I would take a ferry across a sea.
The coach windows beaded with the vapor
Of human warmth. I ran fingers along the jeweled moment
Before it died in the taunting arms of speech.

NIGHT SESSIONS

Why my Korean brothers do not talk
in class, I do not know. They
wait like children around
a piñata, waiting to strike
the teacher's question,
make the world turn
with silencing answers of God.
Late night talks of the eternal
make them sleepy headed for class,
miss the assignments, pull all night sessions
to try and score perfectly, knowing
it is too late, make them work
all the harder, their faces furrowed
the color of ash.

If you don't believe me,
watch them play basketball
at midnight. Stout Korean bodies
flying, making their own
pale light, making the ball rise
like a red moon, a prayer
thrown up to God, leaving books
for exams stacked high behind
in faith, leaving the silence
of parents locked in stores,
shoulders hunched, bowlegged,
exhausted, wondering whether
their children knew—*all this was done for you*—.

How they love this game until dawn,
dark bodies, the soot of asphalt,
thud into one another; the sharp pavement cut
of shoes, piercing the night—the silence
of a basketball leaving the palm—
Better make it a good prayer.

KISS

Saving money the summer
before moving to New York,
I painted houses during days,
nights in a restaurant kitchen
hosing dishes, loading them
into a steel washer that gusted
steam until two a.m.
Once, when I came home,
my back and neck bidding for bed,
asleep on the couch lay Dad.
Flicker from muted TV
was the room's lone light,
but I could see his face fine,
broad nose, thick cheeks
holding glow as he breathed.
In five hours I would wake,
ride in the crew truck
to the assigned site,
gallon buckets and stepladders
chattering over road bumps,
axels clanging
like prongs of a struck fork.
Still, I stood and stared
at Dad, a man
who poured four years
into the Navy during war,
who worked worse
jobs for shorter pay than me,
whose hands have blackened
fixing cars that quit
no matter how many replaced parts.

Above our house, clouds
polished moon as they passed.
Dad wriggled,
body pain or threatening dreams.
What else could I do
but bend down slow
and touch once
my lips to his brown brow?

CELLO SUITE

1

Legions of bending
barberries—witches' capes—
edge the mountain face.
November sun arrows
the gravesite. I hear them
whisper, *go on, we go on*.

2

Memories like ironies
stick: pine sap.
They never come off
but you smell of life.

3

With you lying over me
over the edge, I slip,
still gripping your grip.
With your hand in mine
I reach for your hand
and we palm each other's
fortune into one more day.

4

Why is there a string
in my chest on which a
cello suite is played?
Every breath a downbow?

I know it keeps the player tired;
I know she will stop soon and rest
from so much music.

From *Motherhood Exaggerated*, by Judith Hannan

The morning after her surgery, Nadia is still recognizable, her delicate features not yet swallowed by angry, engorged tissue. Small, swaddled, and bald; eyes shut, multiple umbilical cords connecting her to oxygen, fluid, and drugs, ridding her of waste, blood, and toxins—Nadia is to be reborn. Her challenge is to grow from zero to nine in two weeks. She is not so far out of the first womb that she doesn't remember how.

Seeing...

For her second birth, she has a short trip through the canal separating unconsciousness from awareness. There is only one sign; her eyes open.

Eyes do not tear during surgery because anesthesia paralyzes the body. If the eyes weep, the patient is feeling too much and must be sent deeper. The lids are taped shut; a greasy ointment prevents corneal abrasions.

When Nadia's eyes open, they are not infant eyes. These eyes see; and when they see me, they weep. I have no numbing medicine to combat her tears. I have no power to help at all.

"You don't have to do anything but be there," my friend Maureen, a pediatric anesthesiologist, tells me. "Nadia will always remember that you were there for her." But I am not interested in memories; the present leaves no room for reflection.

Nadia's eyes move beyond me to the nurses who talk to her in nonstop cheery chatter, to the doctors who have come to alleviate pain, to others who cause it. I struggle to interpret what she might be feeling. I don't know where I can touch her because I don't know where it hurts. I can't slap away the hand of the doctor, a clumsy subordinate member of the surgical team, who presses Nadia's jaw too firmly with the probe that checks for a pulse in her newly connected bone. I can't turn the lights low or soothe her with my mother's milk. This is not my labor. This is not my delivery.

For almost two weeks, Nadia's eyes will be my only clue to her moods. With her entire face swollen, her jaw wired shut, her veins infused with morphine, her face expresses nothing. I will have to become a much better reader of irises.

RUNNING BOARDS

Take me riding in your car, car.
—Woody Guthrie

Who remembers running boards when a man
could stand, one foot perched,
peer down
the blouse of his neighbor's wife,

her hand touching his naked arm.
Or the way girls sat on running boards,
trading secrets until,
leaving for work, he shooed them off to school?

Tiptoe, a girl stepped
on the running board of her father's Packard,
turned her cheek for a kiss.
I'll be back soon," he called driving off.

I'll take you riding in my car.
In late afternoon she paced the front stoop.
Miles away, the windshield splintered,
the radio stopped like his heart.

MEMORY BOYS

At my reunion I didn't see any of the guys
I really wanted to see
just a lot of high-school kids
dressed up as middle-aged men
hair missing in a variety of places
and bodies reformed into softer shape
but not the kids I remembered, not the boys
from this all-boys school
the ones in grass-stained football uniforms
or squeaking sneakers on the floor
of the gymnasium
the ones sneaking cigarettes in the graveyard
down the street from the student union
or flipping butter pads to the ceiling
of the dining hall
all I saw were doctors and bankers
and a country club brat or two
some reliving the glory days
complete with poetic license
some still feeling superior after all these years
putting themselves in the hall of fame
I didn't want to talk so much about sports
or school or families or careers
I wanted to talk about the kid who got drunk my senior year
and scaled the slate roof of the dormitory,
gable to gable, four of them, like Spider-Man,
and hopped into the Xavier Hall tower
and rang the bell at three in the morning
with a hunk of steel pipe as if he were Quasimodo
put that motherfucker in the hall of fame.

The Laundress Catches Her Breath, by Paola Corso

FROM STEP BY STEP WITH THE LAUNDRESS

1. It's easier to wash clean clothes if wearing clean clothes, a saying adapted from your college-educated uncle who says it's easier to find a job if you have a job when he hears you chewed out Stubby for cutting back your hours at Eat'n Park.

2. Sort clothes in neat piles on the basement floor beside the safe where your father Mister Twenty Horns stashes company photos from mill picnics and prayer cards for every deceased member of the family, alphabetized by saint.

3. Check pockets for matches, lighters, cigarettes left from break, a string of beads Unc bought for job interviews but you wore to bar bingo and stuffed in a pocket because it felt like bugs around your neck.

4. Load the washer, set the dial, and pour in double the detergent, knowing old man Twenty Horns waters it down since you told him to either stop buying the cheap-ass Giant Eagle brand or you'd quit doing his laundry.

5. As soon as the clothes are submerged in soapy water, have a cigarette and listen to Tom Jones until the line "Whoa, whoa, whoa, she's a lady" or your butt burns out. Whichever comes first.

SCARS

When I pass them in the forgiving field
A woman with a face as brown as earth smiles
And I see the scar across her forehead
And wonder if she was struck by shrapnel
In the rice paddies of Vietnam
Where she and the other women lived
Before they found sanctuary between
These hills in Massachusetts.
They work twenty acres
Without planes dropping napalm
Or rifles stuttering
From the tapestry of trees.
They always wave to me
And probably never consider
How I once carried a rifle
Through the jungles of their country.
I would like to take off my shirt
And show them the scar
On my back, then join them in the field
To work under the sun
In the slow dance of the wind.

Confessions of Joan the Tall: A Memoir, by Joan Cusack Handler

ONLY WATER AND NO PEOPLE

Everywhere around me all the time are walls and rooms and too many people. And there's always someone there in the same room with you folding the wash and doing homework and practicing piano and drums too and drawing and watching TV and cooking dinner and talking on the phone. So if a person wants to do some thinking, they have to find a place where they can be by themselves. That's why the beach when everyone leaves is so great. My favorite thing to do is to sit all the way out at the edge where all I see is Water and no people. It's a game I play every day trying to find the perfect spot where I can't see one living person in front of me or to the left or right when I turn my head.

And Peace and Quiet aren't the only things I love about the Water, I love that it's huge and going on forever and taking me wherever I want to go. But sometimes I don't want to go anywhere, I just want to be right there sitting at the edge of the bulkhead or jetty with the water stretching out all around me like this big beautiful table all glistening and ready for me to spread out all my thoughts. And it's so great having all that space around me with lots of room to stretch my arms and legs and still they won't touch anything. Not one thing. And with all that room, I even feel kind of small. It's true. I mean my body isn't too big for the space like it is in the desks in school which're for midgets not real kids and for sure not Too Tall ones. And the streets in Edgewater where only one car can go through at a time and a million other things that make my body seem like it doesn't fit. So sitting here with all this water stretching out around me makes me feel normal size and cross my heart sometimes even small. Almost like a girl and never in a million years could I ever get tired of that. So I always thank God for being so kind that He gave me the Water. And that isn't even something I prayed for, I never even knew I needed it. But He did, He's always there just watching out for me, deciding what I need then giving it when it's time.

The Waiting Room Reader, Volume II, edited by Rachel Hadas

FROM EDITOR'S NOTE

When I think of people in waiting rooms, including myself, I picture us rifling restlessly through battered magazines. No doubt the image is out of date; these days, we're more likely to be texting or talking on cell phones or playing solitaire on some tiny device. No matter: the nervous impatience of the mood in that room doesn't change. The very situation of waiting, of enduring a period of time of unknown duration in a special place reserved for just such endurance, sends most of us on a skittish quest for news from outside the waiting room. If word about our test results or our loved one's condition isn't immediately available (and if it were, why would we be there?), we turn to speedier bulletins to distract ourselves. Current events, celebrity gossip, auto racing, trout fishing—take your pick, and I haven't even mentioned the TV that's likely to be on. All the while, of course, our minds are busily engaged in a dance of avoidance and dread. It's hard to focus on anything.

There's another sort of waiting as well. This kind, which takes place in nursing homes, involves patience rather than fear. But what both flavors of waiting demand, in their respective styles, is steadfastness—the ability to stick with the situation. In circumstances where we can do little but just be there, it helps to pay attention to something. Paying attention to one particular thing rather than flipping pages or scrolling text prevents us from being distracted and thus, paradoxically, can successfully distract us—can move our minds, if only briefly, from the claustrophobic space and the repetitive scenarios in which we may feel trapped.

This book, the second in the *Waiting Room Reader* series, grows from the belief that one good thing to be able to pay attention to in waiting rooms is poetry. Poems with staying power are always themselves acts of attentiveness, and reading any good poem both demands and rewards attention. The job, then, is to make sure poems can be found in waiting rooms, where they will always be needed. In soliciting work for this book, a book which is intended to find its way into the hands of many people in many waiting rooms, I sought poems whose focused engagement might hook the reader, who, once drawn in, might just lose herself in the poem.

I didn't want narratives (which you get in newspapers and magazines) or conversations (which you get in cell phone or texting exchanges); I wanted nouns. I found myself choosing poems that memorably presented things: beets, a scar, a sweater, a bird's nest, a dog. But of course, poems function like verbs too. All the works in this collection enact longing and memory; they recall, they evoke, they praise. The writing is an act of reclamation, an evocation of some lost original, which isn't so lost after all.

The sixty-three poems and fourteen prose pieces gathered here touch upon themes poets have always visited: memory, family, love, loss, nature. Voices and styles naturally and delightfully vary; some pieces are chiseled and succinct, others loose and rhapsodic. But all, in addition to being accomplished, share the generosity and intensity of their attention to a particular piece of experience. To read through the many submissions and choose the best writers, and then from their work to choose no more than one poem or prose piece per writer (a rule I made for myself), and then to arrange the resulting pile into something like an arc, something like a story, and something like a conversation, was a very pleasurable challenge. It was a task I undertook in the summer and fall of 2011 at a time late in my husband's life when I myself was putting in many hours in ERs and ambulances and waiting rooms. All the more, then, was I reminded of the eloquence of poetry in such places.

It is my ardent hope that the most restless or distracted rifler through these pages may happen upon a poem, a stanza, a line, or an image that will absorb her, remind her, focus her, make her laugh—whatever she needs at that moment. After all, that's how poetry works.

Along with these words, all of us send our thoughts to people in waiting rooms everywhere.

Rachel Hadas
New York City
March 2012

PORTRAIT OF A YOUNG MAN

Lorenzo Lotto, c. 1530

I don't know why the pale sad face
attracts me or why the brown lizard
in the painting looks at him
from a shawl-covered table.

The staid curator says
such sadness was associated
with sensitive temperament

and the pamphlet explains
strewn rose petals
were a cure for melancholy.

The young man's back is turned
from a lute, a hunting horn,
a dead pheasant in the dark background.

A listless hand turns pages
in a book. The face, transfixed and white,
gazes out and down at nothing.
He could be dying—my son had such a pallor.

door of thin skins, by Shira Dentz

CIRCUMFLEX

back up
going nowhere
a trampoline
my father wrangling,
holding me down
to kiss me
when i don't want
to be touched
she screams
anger a splinter
a girl with no sex
his own flesh
and blood
the zero at the center of an egg
nothing happening
—dragonfly body,
transparent as its wings
a dragonfly needle into the heart
needle
i wish i had a piano
to portray the landscape
without hills
without mouths
how the woodenness,
circumflex, tepee
she the wooden dummy inside a shoe
put there to keep its shape
What do you call your father?

beginning with hugs
to unstiffen me
and have me embrace
less standoffishly,
to his sitting beside me
because he was
so *uncomfortable*
with my being
so *uncomfortable*
and *withdrawn*,
to sitting in his lap
to provide me
with a *reparative*
nurturant experience,
to kissing,
tongue-kissing,
to fondling
my breasts,
eventually exposed,
saying, *You think*
I'm doing this for you,
but really
I'm doing it for me,
to the exasperated
fingering
to see if she was
wet.

From *Primary Lessons*, by Sarah Bracey White

When we arrive at the school, Mama goes through the main door into the gymnasium. Butch blows me a kiss as he heads to the gym to await my official arrival. I'm ushered through a side entrance into the locker room where eleven other girls in a wide array of rustling white gowns primp in front of the mirrors. We *ooh* and *aah* over one another's dresses, giddy with excitement and nervousness. "I just hope I don't fall down the stairs when they call my name," says one girl. Everyone laughs, but I have the same fear, even though we've practiced negotiating the six steps down from the platform where we will stand while they call our name and read a statement about us.

When Mrs. McCain announces that they're ready to present us, we form a line according to height and march into the gymnasium. I suddenly get chills and begin to shake. At the back entrance, we're each handed a bouquet of red carnations tied with a wide red streamer that dangles below it. My bouquet dances in my hands. We can hear the rhythms of a live band playing, but the guests are hidden from our view by the large stage that has been built to serve as our launching pad.

One by one, Mrs. McCain sends us up the back stairs onto the platform where we are to stand in the spotlight beneath a wooden trellis covered in red carnations. When it's my turn, she touches my shoulder and says, "Good luck." As I step into the spotlight, a warmth comes over me and my butterflies disappear. I lift my chin and stand tall, unmindful of Mama's frequent warning that the tallest tree always attracts lightning. This night, I feel invincible. I smile as Mrs. McCain told us to do, but I couldn't have done anything else, even if I wanted to. I'm so happy I feel as if I could float down those six steps.

A voice over the loudspeaker says, "Ladies and gentlemen, it is my privilege to present Miss Sarah Marie White, the youngest daughter of Roberta Bracey White and William Edward White." Flashbulbs pop as Mr. E. C. Jones, the local black photographer, snaps pictures from his perch high up on a ladder. I'm happy to have this moment commemorated. The voice continues: "Sarah is sixteen years old and a senior at Lincoln High School, where she is the editor-in-chief of the school newspaper, a member of Quill and Scroll Honor Society, and an on-air school reporter for radio station WDXY. Sarah will attend Morgan State College in the fall."

When the voice stops, I begin my descent toward Butch who is waiting at the bottom step. Applause fills the air. When Butch takes my left hand, I bow to the audience and drop into a deep curtsey, holding it for as long as I can, before straightening up and letting him lead me to my position in a semicircle beside the other girls. He stands behind me, close enough so that I can feel his warm breath on my neck. When the last girl has been introduced and the lights in the gymnasium are turned on, I search the audience for Mama and finally spot her at a table with friends, beaming. I smile in her direction, hoping that I've finally made her happy.

Then the band begins to play *The Blue Danube*. I turn toward Butch, and we assume our dance positions. As our line of dancers slowly circles the highly polished gym floor in a clockwise direction, I'm dizzy with excitement. Butch holds me steady, and I melt into his lead. I can almost feel everyone's eyes following us with approval as we float along on the music. It feels as if we're part of a perfect wheel, moving in perfect form. The crystal ball showers a magnificent array of colors upon us. Tonight, the fact that we're colored doesn't matter. Tonight, I feel like a beautiful princess, smiled upon and feted by people I respect and who respect me. Tonight, I'm more than just another poor little colored girl living in the shadows. I'm filled with the infinite possibilities of who I can become.

My Mother's Funeral, by Adriana Páramo

FROM MARIQUITA

Mom walks toward the cage, unafraid. I hold my breath. How can she be this bold? Doesn't she know how dangerous Margarita is? Stealthily, I climb the mango tree, wrap my legs and arms around one of its branches, steady my body, and peer down at Mom. She leans on the *guadua* fence, looking toward the cage, and something within her seems to break loose. I think she is weeping, and I want to ask why, but then I hear her say, "Poor thing." She opens the gate and walks toward the cage. I expect Margarita to flail at Mom through the bars, to grunt and throw a couple of fiery punches into the air, but she doesn't. Something within her seems to melt.

Mom kneels on the ground, takes hold of the bars with both hands, and begins to whisper to Margarita. I think I hear her singing something slow and sweet, like a lullaby, and then she says, "You can't see it, but I also live in a cage." The two women interlace their fingers. I imagine that they're making a quilt. One brings patches from the drawers of her insanity, whimsical patterns splashed with stolen colors; the other brings patches from hand-me-down clothes, mended socks, and sleepless nights. They look at each other and the rough edges of their faces disappear. They become smooth and fluid like the pebbles of the Gualí River.

Yet I'm concerned about Mom's remark. I can't stand the thought of her being caged. I slip down from the tree and run back to the houses, searching behind doors in one, underneath heavy furniture in the other, frantically looking for a cage. Wherever it is, I'll set Mom free. I'll bring down the bars, I'll destroy the lock, I'll burn the pad, until all that was hard and restraining around her is turned into ashes—soft, powdery, light.

Same Old Story, by Dawn Potter

HOME

So wild it was when we first settled here.
Spruce roots invaded the cellar like thieves.
Skunks bred on the doorstep, cluster flies jeered.
Ice-melt dripped shingles and screws from the eaves.
We slept by the stove, we ate meals with our hands.
At dusk we heard gunshots, and wind and guitars.
We imagined a house with a faucet that ran
From a well that held water. We canvassed the stars.
If love is an island, what map was our hovel?
Dogs howled on the mainland, our cliff washed away.
We hunted for clues with a broken-backed shovel.
We drank all the wine, night dwindled to grey.
    When we left, a flat sunrise was threatening snow,
    But the frost heaves were deep. We had to drive slow.

THE STEAM OF TEA

a pot of tea
  that usual restaurant white ceramic
  with the single restrained dark green equator

in the spread yellow sunlight
  of the February morning
  centers the table with its heat

as she remembers and tells him
  of her father, a pilot,
  taking her at twelve to Paris

how up on the Trocadero
  in the plaza of the Musée de L'Homme
  looking down on the Eiffel Tower

he suddenly took her wrists
  twirled her so fast
  that she became a straight line out

and she learned
  what he wanted to her to learn:
  her complete freedom in the air

and how that brought her
  to a sumptuous freedom on the ground.
  Across the table, he listens to her

and looks behind her
  out the window at the rusted
  railroad bridge over the river

that drains, just here, into the bay.
This is the ramshackle part of town
old pilings, dilapidated docks,

the broken hulk of a ferry
that gives weight
to his falling in love in February.

The Bar of the Flattened Heart, by David Keller

CLASSIFIED

I have radioactive dinner plates. Not because they were exposed
to radiation in Los Alamos, where my father worked, where I
remember guards by what seems a fountain, oh highly unlikely
on the top of that New Mexico mesa, and around a barbed-wire
enclosure, carrying Tommy guns as I waved my father Happy
New Work and Goodbye.

When I heard someone on the radio talk about the orange glaze
on Fiestaware being, like the bomb, made from uranium and
dangerous, that's when I fell in love, and from time to time in
antique stores and junk shops I pick up a plate or two of that color.

They're supposed to be slightly warm from the radioactivity,
but I haven't noticed. My mother knew little of what my father
did in those last years of the war, save that afterwards he disliked
anything radioactive—x-ray machines in shoe stores where you
could stare at the grey bones of your feet moving slowly on the
screen like slugs, and watches with glow-in-the-dark numbers—
both of which delighted my childhood until they too disappeared.

He died of cancer at the age I am now, though that had nothing
to do with his work, him being a theorist and all. My wife says
it seems too fitting, and people I tell nod knowingly about
that work and the bomb, which I think appalled my father. He
switched his field of study after the war. My mother can tell us
nothing of his reasons, but now I have these radioactive plates as
some slightly-warm memory of our family during the orange war,
proud of his work and of some history we could never mention
among ourselves in the way prisoners in the Japanese internment
camps never talk about what happened to them in those years.

My Crooked House, by Teresa Carson

FITTED SHEETS

At the age of fifty-six, I don't know how to fold a fitted sheet. Even worse, I feel folding fitted sheets into small neat rectangles that fit on shelves in an orderly fashion is beyond my abilities. I am not kidding. Every week when the sheets come out of the dryer I start folding with optimism—this time I will surely figure it out—and end with rumpled messes, which spill onto the floor when anyone opens the linen closet door. Every week my belief becomes stronger: I am broken in some fundamental way and thus incapable of learning how to fold a fitted sheet. I trust my ability to understand complex scientific theories such as dark matter or to fix an outage affecting sixty-thousand telephone lines or to travel alone in a foreign country but not my competency with easily-mastered-by-everyone-else-in-the-universe tasks such as applying makeup, buying shoes that fit, blow-drying my hair, managing money, cooking simple meals, housekeeping, or tending a flower garden. It has been this way my whole life. Sure I get by because you can get by with wrinkled sheets in disorderly closets by pretending you're above worrying about such nonsense but, truth be told, week after week I'm in the basement trying to figure it out.

ALTERNATIVE

In the photograph never taken, you're not my
mother, not the woman in the knitted sweater

leaning on the sill. Taller, more secure, you love
language, understand politics, don't give a damn

what folk think. You go to Glasgow Art School,
Mackintosh's palace, become a sculptor—long

emaciated bodies a specialty—have many
lovers, no slave to father, brother. No kids,

but three abortions. The hard confidence finds
something real to do, no fussing over bouquets

for shut-ins, no selling of unripe bananas
at the Eventide Home. You settle in Firenze,

wrong side of the Arno, play guitar, smoke
pastel-colored cigarettes, kiss Tuscan lovers

of both sexes, worry only about your weight.
Wear coral lipstick, jet black mascara, Fendi,

your signature scent. You decide precisely
when, where, and how to die. Keep your

mind fixed on Keats, Etruscan tombs,
avocados, light on the water, apricots.

Misery Islands, by January Gill O'Neil

ZEBRA

for my son

You are not who they say you are.
You are Nubian with white stripes

and sport a Mohawk for a mane.
Once hunted to extinction,

your deafening bray is a song for the fallen.
Some might even say you are God's mistake.

But how ordinary the world would be without you.
They will say stay in your herd, stick close to your mother's side.

Remember, you are all equine.
Put another way, you are a wild ass.

Raise those ears. Kick your legs.
Gaze that impenetrable stare.

Your forefathers once grazed on African grasses.
Your place in this world is the one you claim.

Places I Was Dreaming, by Loren Graham

EPISODE OF THE ENCYCLOPEDIA SALESMAN

I knew better than to ask for things we couldn't afford
and even at seven had taught myself not to want them— but I wanted
those books with the red rectangles on their spines, Colliers'
huge black volumes that the stranger extracted
from his black case and lined up on our linoleum.
I knew Grandma
thought he had a gun in there, what she always thought
about strangers like this one in shiny black shoes and white
shirt and dark tie, who sat on the flowered yellow
kitchen chair next to our coal stove.
And I knew Dad
would say *no, we can't pay for them*, that Mom would say *no,*
they're free at the library, that my smart aleck cousin
would ask *Why don't you show us some big heavy books?*

I was wrong, though: Dad looked straight at me.
There's an old car I could overhaul that would bring the money
if you think you could use these.
The room got quiet.
I waited for Uncle Fred to say something like *Hell,*
if he reads all them, he'll be purt near smart as me.
But the silence held, a first in that house,
so I just mumbled *Yessir, I spect I could*,

as though I had no idea, even at seven,
of what my *yessir* meant to everyone present:
another month of beans, less coal for the fire,
my father's spending his winter evenings with a drop light
in the unheated barn he used for a garage—
the real price of privilege, its great black bulk.

JANUARY 2009: FOR ANTHONY

thirty weeks

As if to herald your coming, miracles
on the nightly news. A woman gives birth
to octuplets: in California, her nursery
holds eight wooden cribs
for the preschool class
conceived in a lab and implanted
aboard the minuscule school bus
of her uterus.

A plane sets down on the Hudson.
Passengers of US Airways 1549
stand on the aircraft's wings,
and though I know it's all physics
and well-trained flight attendants,
they walk on water.

In the frigid air of the Capitol steps,
a man born at the crossroads
of Kansas and Kenya
takes the oath of office. A historic first.
Next day, a historic second—
the man sworn in all over again
since the black robe bungled his lines.

These, Anthony, are the everyday
wonders that pass for news, and history,
that, inching toward the vanishing point
of time, all become trivia
or less, molecules, hydrogen and oxygen
rushing downriver to join the ocean.

If I have wisdom,
it’s this: question miracles
and believe,
for you are one
and you aren’t.

Esther: A Novel in Verse, by Pam Bernard

FROM GREAT DIVIDE

The two huddled there until the storm
gathered its robes and headed off.
Raymond slowly lowered his arms,
stared straight ahead, unblinking.

Esther spoke to him quietly.
You're here with me, she whispered,
not sure what else to say, or why she felt
so odd. He turned to her then, a peculiar
restlessness working his jaw,
and when he saw her bloodied face,

the gash above her brow, he opened
his mouth in horror, but only a rasping
came from his lungs.

Esther sat motionless, her hand
on Raymond's shoulder. Tears and blood
rivered down her cheek, though
she did not yet feel the pain.

Some time passed before Raymond
took out his handkerchief and gently
unfolded it. Then, as if he'd forgotten what
he meant to do with it, he folded it again,
stuffed the cloth back into his breast pocket.

He started the car and began the drive
down the windward side of the mountain
as if nothing at all had happened.

Esther's hand fell limp to her lap.

LEAVING

Not to be here anymore, not to hear
The cat's fat purring, not to smell
Wood smoke, wet dog, cheap cologne, good cologne,
Not to see the sun and stars, oaks

And asters, snow and rain, every form
I take mostly for granted, makes me sad
But pleased to be writing down these words,
Pleased to have been one more who got the chance

To participate, who raised his hand although
He didn't know the answer or understand
The question. No matter. The leaving makes me sad;
So much was offered, so freely and completely.

Only So Far, by Robert Cording

ANGEL

Yesterday's tragedy is today's entertainment
on YouTube. Less than a day old,
this two-minute clip from last night's news
has over a million hits. Everyone's watching
Angel, a seventy-eight-year-old man hit by
a car that sped away, lying in the street
in downtown Hartford, blocks from
the Capitol dome, the half-gallon of milk
he was carrying broken on the pavement.
It's lunchtime, a cloudless summer day,
pigeons moping on the sidewalks, passersby
carrying off Styrofoam cartons of take-out.

What's got everyone watching is the number
of pedestrians who come to the curbside, look,
and rush away, hands in their pockets,
heads down, now and again looking back.
Two send a text to a friend, another
takes a picture on her cell. Six continue to wait
for their bus, watching as cars carefully
half-circle the elderly man, then zip away.

And there is someone whom we cannot see,
who filmed this street full of people and sold it
to the local station. And here I am,
replaying this scene, counting the people
on the street as if each one of them bears
some failure of my own. And there's that
ghostly bruise of milk leaking out like some kind
of divine substance, a would-be revelation.

The Baby Book, by Robin Silbergleid

AN OPEN LETTER TO FRIDA KAHLO

When my legs were dumb from the D&C,
when my feet were heavy, stirrupped balls of cotton
& I couldn't tell where they stopped & the blankets began,
I thought of you.
                    They kept putting more blankets on me—
they were white & everyone else wore green, my doctor
in her scrubs standing between my legs. I'd been there
before, in your painting dear Frida,
& there were wires attached to my chest & there were tubes
run between my legs, & Dr. E sucked it out, him out,
my boy, I mean, & I thought if this scene were a painting
by Frida Kahlo it would be beautiful, & I laughed.
The sound filled the room like a newborn's cry.
Frida, what I wanted to say is that I understand
why you come back to this room, a hospital in Detroit,
why the paintings pin you there to the bed like a bug on a nail,
because you're still there.
                              You left pieces of yourself behind—
a blot on a sheet, some tissue in a jar—& you want them back.

Orphans, by Joan Cusack Handler

FROM INOPERABLE

One by one, we came,
each emerging from her dark appraisal — for there was
nothing of that harsh branding now. All guile gone —
only smiles, as many jokes as she could conjure,
abundant words of each one's worth.
It took till she was dying
for her to know we loved her.
And dare I say it,
she seemed happy — I too
grateful for the gift
of this cancer, my last
chance to convince her —
yet even now, my hand hesitates,
reluctant to write
how deeply
I love her.

Eating Moors and Christians, by Sandra M. Castillo

PHOTOGRAPH

with respect for Omar Lara

1.
I am the six-year-old in the center, the timekeeper in the Havana-blue dress, waving as if to say *Adios Habana,* the birthday girl sitting on the lacquer-black coffee table Mother dragged out to *el portal* for the afternoon, two years before we lose everything. But there is no way of knowing any of this as *Tío* Berto measures the existing light, the distance between me and the inevitable, mapping our lives with photographs.

2.
The red and green *croto* plants framing the shot: Teroina's house behind me, its wooden green Caribbean windows shut tight, a skeleton inside, Dyango singing between our lives about geography or distance, about what you cannot forget—the color of grief—language pressed between flesh and nostalgia as she wastes away from love or cancer, the past lost or unreachable.

3.
Here, at the edge of the afternoon, I cast my own shadow, myself as Other, the dark daguerreotypes *de mis antepasados, cafetaléros, Españoles, Isleños, generaciones perdidas*, not yet lost, destroyed, cut into fragments, the mosaic pieces of the past, our ancestry, along with the passport pictures *de mi Abuela* Isabel, *mi Abuelo* Leopoldo, that might expose those who will choose to stay behind, imagining that they will always be themselves here, where everything is familiar and that we will never return to this life, this long summer house, so haunted with whispers, so filled with the scent of olive oil and garlic, to find how little survives.

Tornadoesque, by Donald Platt

THIS HAPPENED

A shepherd in Afghanistan spotted
a young girl's head lying in the new grass.

He wanted to bury it, give her soul
rest. He picked her head up, gazed for one

moment straight into her open brown eyes.
It weighed ten kilos. Too heavy, he thought.

Next second it exploded. His five sons
could find no body parts to wash, anoint,

say the old words over, bury. Allah,
be merciful to him, her, them, us all.

READING TO MY KIDS

When they were little I read
to them at night until my tongue
got tired. They would poke me
when I started to nod off after twenty pages
of Harry Potter or Lemony Snicket.
I read (to them) to get them to love reading
but I was never sure if it was working
or if it was just what I was supposed to do.
But one day, my daughter (fifteen then)
was finishing *Of Mice and Men* in the car
on our way to basketball.
She was at the end when I heard her say,
No, in a familiar frightened voice
and I knew right away where she was.
"Let's do it now," Lennie begged,
"Let's get that place now."
"Sure, right now. I gotta. We gotta,"
and she started crying, then I started crying,
and I think I saw Steinbeck
in the back seat nodding his head,
and it felt right to me,
like I'd done something right,
and I thought to myself, *Keep going,*
read it to me, please, please, I can take it.

PORTRAIT WITH CLOSED EYES

She was the stain in the teacup
that spread up toward the handle.
She was the handle that snapped
off the hairbrush, and
She was the hairbrush he tossed
onto the fire, and
She was the fire he carried
each day in his pipe.

She was the pipe the bath water
rode to the river, and
She was the river where they
boarded the boat to limbo.
She was the limbo that held
the secrets of acorns, and
She was the acorn that
bruised his weary knees.

She was the knees that knocked
beneath the oak table, and
She was the table where glasses
were refilled till midnight.
She was the midnight that darkened
the brow of the child,
Child who never felt safe indoors,
who never felt safe outdoors.

She, the heaviest of doors, was the reason.
She was their stain.

A CAR STOPS AND A DOOR OPENS

The first time I hadn't expected
a thing so momentous
would take so little time.
When I got out of the car, I was surprised
to find street lamps looked the same,
though they didn't seem interested
in shedding light. It was all I could do
not to stop strangers
and tell them everything, as one might
after being abducted by aliens
and subject to experiments.
At home, I thought even the cat would guess
I was not the same boy
who'd fed her just before leaving.
I was tempted to brag to my brother.
Finally, here was something I'd done
he hadn't. The second time it happened
I realized how lucky I was
to have survived the first. I watched
the car drive off and stood in a downpour
and let myself be hit again
and again by the obliging rain.
There was no third time. The car stopped
and I didn't get in.

YAWP

Read this love letter to life. Its pages turn in the ice-fling
off of the fast car's roof. Follow the traveling carillon,
the communism of the gospels, the ice rink's joyful
four-fold spotlight, how it shines the hair and adds grace.

Eyes and words swerve into focus, nouns marry in metaphor,
lines enter a stranger's memory and stay for seven years.

Smell the multiflora roses, honeysuckle, burning leaves.
Feel the inside of the body, the smooth core, watch the wren
pull the dead fledgling from the hole feather by dusty feather.
Guess the stories: tailless squirrel on the woodpile, condom

under the old folks home sofa, the lady's internal monologue
as she guards the Lamborghini at the auto show, red guts spilt

like berries from rabbit mouth. I'd write even if each page's
only destination were the stove, for winter heat. Again and again.

Miss August, by Nin Andrews

GOD'S MISTAKE (GIL)

God makes mistakes. Even as a boy, I knew. I hated how everyone says God is perfect and great and all that kind of stuff. I wanted to say to them, Look around, why don't you? Look at all the folks who aren't who they say they are. Not a bit like it. All the sick folks, all the ugly folks, all the mean folks, all the folks who look half-baked. All the folks who think if they can just get a new hairdo, a new car, a new dishwasher, they'll be just fine, thank you very much. I feel sorry for them. I really do.

Sometimes I wonder if anyone feels okay in their own skin. Nobody wants to admit they're all wrong. So they make up stories. Or pray. Or lie. Or they drink cocktails at five o'clock. Like my daddy did. Whiskey on the rocks. Lots of whiskey. Not many rocks. It doesn't make a man into somebody else. Just makes him mean.

Me? I don't pretend. I blame God. I say, *God, you made one big old mistake when you made Gil Simmons*. But he won't answer me. You know how God is.

CHELSEA PIERS

My lover and I stroll down the piers,

post pescatarian dinner, in midsummer.

He points to the moon, veiled by clouds.

The Hudson River murmurs soft waves.

Across, the buildings glitter like theater.

Our arms damp, lamps lend themselves

to fantasy of the last two men on earth.

But as I reach for his hand, he pulls it

away, looks hurriedly around. Suddenly

I stand awash in brutal history, periphery

of sanctuary and danger. We are those

punished for our affections. The silent

seagulls disguised as larks. His denial

plunges silver-finned into the river.

Gloved Against Blood, by Cindy Veach

HOW A COMMUNITY OF WOMEN

Resolved, That we will not go back into the mills to work
unless our wages are continued . . . as they have been.
Resolved, That none of us will go back, unless they receive us all as one.
Resolved, That if any have not money enough to carry them home,
they shall be supplied.
—*Boston Evening Transcript*, February 18, 1834

How my French-Canadian great-grandmother and great-great-aunts toiled thirteen hours a day in the textile mills of Lowell, Massachusetts. How weak the light when they left the boardinghouse each morning. How screaming starlings flash mobbed them along the way. How they sucked thread through the eye of their foot-long wooden shuttles that fed the cotton to the looms. How they called that quick motion of their lips "the kiss of death." How they could not converse over the cacophonic, clickety-click, clickety-clack of five-hundred howling looms. How they walked back in ear-ringing darkness, had dinner, then took up their needlework—crochet, crewel, cross-stitch, knitting, mending, quilting, darning—close work, women's work. My mother taught me, her mother taught her, her mother taught her.

WORKS, by Danny Shot

ALLYSON,

I felt bad today for telling you
that Kanye's "Bound 2"
was the worst song I ever heard.

You said you really liked it
and said no more than that,
though I know you were annoyed.

I went home and listened
to it again and again and
again.

Three times.
I didn't watch the video.
I just listened.

I still don't love it.
But I don't hate it either.

I realized being young,
or not too old means
listening with fresh ears,

being able to hear the beauty
or truth that someone else
can hear.

Somehow, I forgot that.
Thanks for the reminder.

Danny

See the Wolf, by Sarah Sousa

TO THE COMEDIAN WHO CALLED THELMA AND LOUISE TWO WHITE HEIFERS

My mother dreamed of wrenching jaws open with her small hands.
I could see it gave her some pleasure. A pleasure
all women share imagining their strength in the face of danger.
My moments as prey were too recent,
I didn't wear the dog's hide beneath my clothes
for power. Though he had been *put to sleep*,
no one offered it to me. I wore an ugly scar
from seventeen stitches, a tender pink
entry wound newly sealed, a mark
that said *good eating*. I startled every time I heard
a keychain jingle: *dog loose*. I'd climb my mother like a tree.
If the dog materialized, worse, if it advanced, growling,
my mother would stand in front of me, arms splayed,
as if she were guarding someone
in a basketball game. But she wasn't fucking around.
My mother had practiced the maneuvers in her sleep,
the way she'd grasp the upper jaw with her right hand,
the lower with her left, and leverage her weight
at the hinges to crack the skull wide like a bivalve shell.
Don't laugh. Women have driven off cliffs,
burned men in their beds, to escape.
Her body over my body, my mother and the dog would face off.
I could feel the answering growl start deep inside her,
erupting in a voice not my mother's,
a voice to make us larger than we were. *Stronger
than a scream*, she'd said. A man laughed at us once.
But it wasn't him the dog obeyed.

Practicing the World, by Judith Sornberger

THIS AUTUMN MORNING ARRAYS ITSELF

in layers of sheer mist before
the almost naked mountain
like a bride in a distant century
preparing to wed the man
she did not choose, yet wrapping
her shy skin in one layer
of silk over another,
slowly—a bird folding
in her wings after flight.
Finally adding her finest kimono—
dove gray stained
with crimson maple leaves—
and tying herself
with an obi of the same
burning apricot as the oak
wears outside my window.

Autumn is always an elegy—
even this one, after living
thirty years with the man
I choose again each morning,
waking in his arms folded
around me like a gown
that knows my body perfectly,
embracing and forgiving
every imperfection.
Then comes the moment
when I step, alone,
into the chill of late October,
the dress rehearsal for
what comes next.

My Oceanography, by Harriet Levin

SMOKE

If I could use smoke as a medium,
I'd have no trouble creating great art.

Strands of clove-scented smoke pull me in layer
by layer amid the mesmerizing sound

of rain hitting the roof,
sidling across the windshield and draining off the hood.

I tilt my head back and imagine
a cigarette pressed against my lover's lips.

Three more left in the pack.
This is the last of him.

Smoke fills my mouth,
passes down my throat and into

my lungs where it infiltrates
every cell in my bloodstream.

I smoke past the red line on the tip,
his body's imprint—

jawline, nape, neck—
tuck the stub into my jean's pocket

for his scent to seep through,
linger, live in my pocket as a remnant,

as I throw open the car door,
step forward and out of him.

HOODIE

A gray hoodie will not protect my son
from rain, from the New England cold.

I see the partial eclipse of his face
as his head sinks into the half-dark

and shades his eyes. Even in our
quiet suburb with its unlocked doors,

I fear for his safety—the darkest child
on our street in the empire of blocks.

Sometimes I don't know who he is anymore
traveling the back roads between boy and man.

He strides a deep stride, pounds a basketball
into wet pavement. Will he take his shot

or is he waiting for the open-mouthed
orange rim to take a chance on him? I sing

his name to the night, ask for safe passage
from this borrowed body into the next

and wonder who could mistake him
for anything but good.

Sweet World, by Maureen Seaton

SWEET WORLD

Wonder what I'd be today if I was still married to my Wall Street
husband besides married to a Wall Street husband and puking gin

in a silk sheath outside Delmonico's. I might be a size 4. I might
be a secret Democrat or a weekend lesbian. This morning five planes

flew over the yard in a V as I was about to dig into a pile of lavender
pancakes al fresco. The V flew low and slow. It flew loud and ominous.

It alarmed me, sounding a lot like the war movies of my fifties' childhood.
My cranky Chihuahua was proverbially biting at flies and I sat there

not thinking about hate. Recently, I experienced life with cancer. An
intoxicating time, richly infused with the liquor of death, but good too

because no one expected much of me and I was left to my own mind,
which is what I'm missing most these days. Unless that's it over there,

screeching on two wheels around the racetrack. Today I typed *gnos*
instead of *song* and I wondered if it was some new app designed

to mess with me. I've never thought to call the world sweet before.
Surviving something can do that, make things taste different.

Suddenly you're a hero/ine. All this devastation—
and you're still standing in the middle of it.

SPLITTING WOOD

It was the thought of his entering
their infant's room that drove her.

She remembered his face the first time
she saw him. Now, half gone from whiskey,
eyes hooded like a hawk's,
he said he'd kill the children when he woke.

The neighbors heard it,
the screams. They heard.

His workman's hand,
his gnarled hand dangled down.
The knife lay by the bed.
She slipped from the covers
while he slept, placed her feet
on the floorboards just so.

The dogs barked outside, snapdragons,
flowered tongues, and all the wired
faces of the past strung up. The ax
hung on the porch, woodpile nearby,
each log plotted, uneasily entwined.
The children's tears were rain,
tears were watering the parched hills.

The wild moon foamed at the mouth.
The wild moon crept softly at her feet.

The arms that grabbed the ax
were not her own,
that hugged it to her heart

while he slept were not hers,
the cold blade sinking in his skin.
She grew up in the country splitting wood.
She knew just how much it took
to bring a limb down.

TAKING MY TIME

Woke up to the sound of rain. Two eggs on toast
And a cup of coffee, a cat napping
On the news. In my robe on a Tuesday morning,
The sound of the rain like typing on the lawn.

The coughing starts early today, each hitch,
Each hiccup, a jolt. In an hour I will be in the office
Of my GP, going over the radiology results.
But for now, I can imagine the outcome

Any way I like. Sunny side up. Early sounds
Of traffic whir, tires splashing up oily waves
At the curb. I can still pretend that I have not already
Read the report. If I sit still and quiet, the coughing

Subsides. If I drink the coffee, slowly. If I take care
Not to wake the children. In the kitchen, the dishes
In a tipsy pile, each plate uncertain, like each day.

AFTER

Well, we're older now. Nothing new
there. We did and yet didn't know
from that very first *I do* how we'd follow
the years toward *who will bury who?*

So tell me again, when our lives are done,
that we'll be together. It's okay
if you lie to me. That's a price I'll pay
for our marriage to continue after we're gone.

Say it, please. Say how it will always be
when we meet again. After everything
we made together is torn apart, nothing
left of us but this paper wish. Tell me.

Truth Has a Different Shape, by Kari L. O'Driscoll

FROM BY HEART

I didn't think that I could ever forget all of those parenting moments that other people take the time to meticulously record in baby books. As they were all happening—first haircut, first tooth lost in a trickle of pink, first pair of shoes—I was certain that every detail would remain lodged in my heart and mind, carbon copies for all time.

I know better now, and I wish I had done a better job marking those occasions. I think about the curious way Mom has lost certain memories and the way she denied other ones, and it makes me want to know how much influence my subconscious has over which things stick and which don't. Perhaps regular moments that are not imbued with emotion, threaded through with fear or anger or fierce love, simply glance off my brain like rocks skipped on the surface of a lake. But the memories encumbered by passion and sentiment sink into my psyche, imprinting themselves on the silty soil beneath and leaving a trail of pebbles for me to turn over and look at whenever I want to. The moments I recall most vividly are the ones whose airy pockets are stuffed with rank, sweaty fear, or a desperate desire to be anywhere other than where I was.

I recall Lauren's eyes, liquid with terror as violent stomach cramps nearly turned her inside out, thanks to a serious allergic reaction. She was certain she was going to die right there at Disneyland, vomiting over and over again into the bushes outside Pirates of the Caribbean.

I will never forget the night six-year-old Erin held our cat while the veterinarian injected him with the poison that would put him to sleep. Her lower lip quivered and tears gathered in the corners of her eyes, but she was determined to be brave. I was simultaneously awed and heartbroken.

I haven't forgotten those moments where I wished for the power to obliterate their pain.

There are moments from my childhood that I am certain were pure emotion, that consisted almost entirely of a fogbank of fear or loathing, but it occurs to me that Mom may not have felt the same way, either because she didn't allow herself to or because of her perspective.

There are experiences that hid from me for decades and later surfaced for reasons I can't comprehend. Why did I remember Clayton molesting me so many years later, and why are there still so many holes? The things I have been able to remember are scattered and scrambled. Timelines cross and bend, and images appear like still photos in a slide show—moments that I see with a singular clarity but cannot fit into a particular place with any certainty. Did those memories hurtle down toward the lake bottom of my mind with enormous speed, propelled by the sheer weight of emotion, and bury themselves so deeply that it took years to uncover them?

Eleanor, by Gray Jacobik

20

I do not advocate the way Franklin handles
personal feelings he would
rather not deal with. Convinced that anything
ignored for a sufficient time
resolves itself, when emotions threaten to
turn disagreeable, he leaves
the room turning to say, *you will feel*
differently when you calm down,
or *you are looking at this in the wrong light.*
Although it is horrid to feel
all bottled up, I do think it essential,
at times, to force one's self to not
think of certain things. We both inherited
the legacy of self-containment
our daughter, Anna, railed against. It makes
true intimacy impossible
for one must never admit to feeling helpless
or weak. I could be every bit
as controlled, when need be, as Franklin was.
This was the Roosevelt way:
individuals of superior breeding must never
in public, and rarely in private,
let bubbling vats of maggoty rage, or sorrow,
or dread or frustration, come
to the surface. Fearless, confident, and cheerful:
always the order of the day.

Scraping Away, by Fred Shaw

ARGOT

In the sweaty restaurant kitchen,
where I'll learn to cuss in Mexican,
tattooed line cooks talk shit in voices
nicked as the bone-white
monkey bowls we stack and fill.

They call the boss and picky customers
chupacabra, "goat sucker,"
being the inside joke
for every pain in the ass.

Years ago, in a place once a mustard factory,
I was a boy touring Mom's latest food-prep gig,
a windowless world where the clam chowder
paddled around in vats
deep enough for me to stand,

and I wore a paper hat,
same as the mustached men in bloody aprons
who cut up and kidded while they hacksawed
T-bones from beef sides.

Now, I'm digging twelve-hour grooves
of full trays in spaghetti joints
with family names. I'm keeping ice bins full
and counters clean, wondering, at times,

if the routine has replaced the oxygen
of my dreams with a working life
that takes what it wants, stealing my pen
and handing me
bad math on credit slips.

On her days off,
Mom wants to play Scrabble,
but instead, we talk about our fingers,
how they've split into open-flowered nerves,
stinging our bodies to the bulk

of a weary self at the end of the day,
each of us searching
for the phrase that captures what it is
to feel at once,
both capable and small.

Set in Stone, by Kevin Carey

SET IN STONE

A rosary that was my mother's
tucked in the glove compartment of his car
and a copy of *Exile on Main St.*
with instructions to play track 6
when he hit some lonesome desert highway.
I love him so much my chest hurts,
thinking of him riding off into his own life,
me the weeping shadow left behind (for now).
I know I'll see him again but it's ceremony
we're talking about after all—
one growing up and one growing older
both wild curses.
A train blows its horn,
the light rising beyond the harbor,
a dog barks from a car window,
and the nostalgia (always dangerous)
hits me like a left hook.
I'm trapped between the memory
and the moment,
the deal we make
if we make it this long,
the markers of a life,
the small worthwhile pieces
that rattle around in my pockets,
waiting to be set somewhere in stone.

BEAD

I still have the shirt he wore to the doctor
the day she took both his hands
and looked into his milky eyes
and told him
as if it were some kind of blessing.

None of us cried, none of that—instead
we sat in an awkward huddle and skimmed
the scan report, all seven single-spaced pages
making no sense, especially to him,
who swore to God

that a life was a string of beads
made of single bright days,
and all you needed to do to be happy
was thread them, now and then hold your strand
up to whatever light there was, but always

keep a firm grip on the bead
you were passing your red string through
that very moment. Then go back
to your stringing, and go back
again, until they were gone.

A DOZEN SECRETS FROM GOD

A baby giggles, on average, 400 times a day.

I can help you add sand to your hourglass.

Church has gotten me wrong.

Think of me more as the cutest thing possible,
as if your all-time favorite dogs time-traveled and had a puppy,
and raising me gently is your only job.

I am the one exclamation point hidden in your encyclopedia.

In my next universe, hummingbirds will sound like thumb pianos.

I am that fountain you didn't have time to visit
at the hilltop castle garden, and you probably won't be back,
but you remember it more clearly than if you had thrown coins in.

Caution: low flying owls, and expectations.

Count how often each year you let rain fall on your face.

When your dog is listening to you, he's not frustrated.
He doesn't wish he knew what you are saying. You sound to him
the way birds sound to you. You're simply chirping.

The stars are just glints shining through a blurry lens;

I am the big thing shining behind.

And you, you are wine for the eyes.

GRATITUDES

It takes a village is an apt description of the scores of CavanKerry board members, staff, and contractors who have joined together to raise CavanKerry Press from birth in 2000 to young adulthood in 2020. Without the combined gifts of her extended family, CavanKerry would not have developed into the jewel that she is. We are deeply indebted to each of you for your exquisite care.

Countless people have contributed to CavanKerry's well-being during the past twenty years. We have done our best to build a comprehensive list here, but memory and records are at best incomplete. We apologize for any omissions and remain ever-grateful to everyone who has been a part of our story.

CavanKerry's Godparents
Florenz Eisman: Beloved Managing Editor 2000–2013
Molly Peacock: Senior Advisor 2000–Present
Baron Wormser: Manuscript Editor, Senior Advisor 2000–Present

Staff & Contributors
Joan Cusack Handler: Founder, Publisher, Senior Editor 2000–Present
Gabriel Cleveland: Managing Editor 2018–Present
Jonathan Spinner, PhD: Development Director, Board Liaison 2018–Present
Dimitri Reyes: Marketing & Communications Director 2019–Present
Elena Neoh: Social Media Assistant 2020–Present
Joy Arbor, PhD: Copy Editor 2019–Present
Teresa Carson: Curator: "La Poesia"; CKP Blogger 2020–Present
Fred Courtright: Permissions 2014–Present
Ryan Scheife: Book Designer 2016–Present

Board of Directors
José Angel Araguz, PhD
Cornelius Eady

Declan Spring
Afaa Michael Weaver
Danny Shot (Previously)

Former Staff & Contributors
Teresa Carson: Associate Publisher 2010–2016
Starr Troup: Managing Editor 2013–2018
Jen Abrams: Grant Writer
Kiersten Armstrong: Website Design
Jenna Beck: Social Media Coordinator
Catherine Breitfeller: Financial Manager
Richard Foerster: Copy Editor
Jamie Parker: Logo Design
Dawn Potter: Copy Editor
Donna Rutkowski: Administrator
Angela Santillo: Marketing
Robert Weibezahl: Press Releases

Former Designers
Peter Cusack
Charles Martin
Greg Smith

CAVANKERRY PRESS AUTHORS

Nin Andrews - Nin Andrews grew up on a farm in Charlottesville, Virginia. She received her BA from Hamilton College and her MFA from Vermont College. Her poems and stories have appeared in many literary journals and anthologies including *Agni*, *Ploughshares*, and *Best American Poetry*. The recipient of two Ohio Arts Council grants, she is the author of many books including *Miss August*, *The Book of Orgasms*, *Southern Comfort*, and *Why God Is a Woman*.

Christian Barter - Christian Barter works at Acadia National Park as a stone worker, rigger, arborist, and trail crew supervisor. Recent poetry has appeared in *Tin House*, *New Letters*, and on poets.org. He has won a Hodder Fellowship from Princeton, and the Maine Literary Award. His latest book is *Bye-Bye Land* from BOA Editions.

Jeanne Marie Beaumont - Jeanne Marie Beaumont is author of *Letters from Limbo* (CavanKerry Press, 2016), *Burning of the Three Fires*, *Curious Conduct*, and *Placebo Effects*, winner of the National Poetry Series. In 2019, her play *Asylum Song* premiered at the HERE Theater in New York. She teaches at the 92nd St. Y.

Pam Bernard - Pam Bernard, poet, professor, and editor, received her MFA from the Program for Writers at Warren Wilson College, and BA from Harvard University. Her awards include a NEA Fellowship and two Mass Cultural Council Fellowships. She has published three full-length collections of poetry, and a verse novel entitled *Esther*.

Bhisham Bherwani - Bhisham Bherwani studied fine arts at New England College. He is also a graduate of New York University and Cornell University, and the recipient of fellowships and scholarships from the Bread Loaf Writers'

Conference, New England College, and the Frost Place. He was born in Bombay, India; he lives in New York City.

Celia Bland - Celia Bland's three collections of poetry were the subject of an essay by Jonathan Blunk in the summer 2019 issue of the *Georgia Review*. *Cherokee Road Kill* (Dr. Cicero, 2018) featured pen and ink drawings by Japanese artist Kyoko Miyabe. The title poem received the 2015 Raynes Prize. Her work is included in *Native Voices: Indigenous American Poetry, Craft and Conversation* (Tupelo Press, 2019). Bland is coeditor with Martha Collins of the essay collection *Jane Cooper: A Radiance of Attention* (University of Michigan, 2019). She is the author of young adult biographies of the Native American leaders Pontiac, Osceola, and Peter MacDonald (Chelsea House Books). Originally from the Blue Ridge Mountains of North Carolina, Bland teaches poetry at Bard College, where she is associate director of the Bard College Institute for Writing & Thinking.

Annie Boutelle - Annie Boutelle, born and raised in Scotland, was educated at the University of St. Andrews and New York University. She teaches in the English Department at Smith College, where she founded the Poetry Center. She lives with her husband in western Massachusetts.

Andrea Carter Brown - Andrea Carter Brown is the author of *The Disheveled Bed* (CavanKerry Press, 2006) and two chapbooks, *Domestic Karma* (Finishing Line Press, 2018) and *Brook & Rainbow* (winner of the Sow's Ear Press Chapbook Prize, 2001). *September 12*, her collection of award-winning poems about 9/11 and its aftermath, is forthcoming in 2021 for the twentieth anniversary of 9/11. Currently, she is series editor of the Word Works Washington Prize. An avid birder, she lives in Los Angeles where she grows lemons, limes, oranges, and tangerines in her backyard.

Eloise Bruce - Eloise Bruce is a member of Cool Women Poets and recipient of the NJ Governor's Award for Arts Education. She has held various roles at the Frost Place. Since its inception she has been integral in nurturing and guiding Poetry Out Loud in NJ and is youth editor for *RavensPerch Magazine*. A chapbook, *Scud Cloud*, a conversation in poetry with her husband David Keller about living with his dementia, is due out in 2020 from Ragged Sky.

Christopher Bursk - A recipient of NEA, Guggenheim, and Pew Fellowships, Christopher Bursk is the author of sixteen books, including *A Car Stops and a Door Opens*, *Dear Terror*, *The Infatuations and Infidelities of Pronouns*, *Cell Count*, and *The Improbable Swervings of Atoms* (winner of the Donald Hall Prize for Poetry from AWP). Most important, he is the grandfather of six, and has three imaginary friends, Wobbly, Oliver, and Nobody.

Kevin Carey - Kevin Carey is the coordinator of creative writing at Salem State University. He is also a filmmaker and playwright. His latest documentary film, *Unburying Malcolm Miller,* about a deceased Salem, MA poet, premiered at the Mass Poetry Festival in 2016. His latest play, "The Stand or Sal Is Dead," a murder mystery comedy, opened in Newburyport, MA at the Actor's Studio on June 21–24, 2018. Kevincareywriter.com.

Teresa Carson - Teresa Carson holds an MFA in poetry and an MFA in theatre, both from Sarah Lawrence College. She is the author of three collections of poetry: *Elegy for the Floater* (CavanKerry Press, 2008); *My Crooked House* (CavanKerry Press, 2014), which was a finalist for the Paterson Poetry Prize; *The Congress of Human Oddities* (Deerbrook Editions, 2015). She is a co-founder of the Unbroken Thread[s] Project, which explores how histories/myths/memories are excavated, interpreted, transformed, and transmitted. She brings poetry to everyone in Sarasota County, Florida through her Poetry in Un/Expected Places project.

Sandra M. Castillo - Born in Havana, Cuba, Sandra M. Castillo left the island of her birth with her family in the summer of 1970 on one of the last of President Johnson's Freedom Flights and grew up in South Florida. Her work explores issues of memory, history, gender, and language, but it reflects a personal vision, tied primarily by history, personal and otherwise. She depicts contradictory worlds, the memory of a homeland, and memory politics while examining the ordinary reality of exile as well as the duality of existence.

Karen Chase - Karen Chase lives in western Massachusetts. She is the author of two collections of poems, *Kazimierz Square* and *BEAR*, as well as *Jamali-Kamali*, a book-length homoerotic poem that takes place in Mughal India. Her award-winning book, *Land of Stone*, tells the story of her work with a silent young man in a psychiatric hospital where she was the hospital poet. Her memoir, *Polio Boulevard,* came out in 2014, followed by *FDR on His Houseboat: The Larooco Log, 1924–1926* in 2016.

David S. Cho - David S. Cho was born and raised in the Chicago area, along with his brother and extended family, the proud children of Korean immigrants in the early 1970s. As an Asian American, he is a man of many homes, balancing his American, Asian immigrant, and Asian American heritage. He has also lived, studied, and taught in Champaign-Urbana, Chicago, Seattle, and west-central Indiana, currently splitting time between western Michigan, and Naperville, Illinois, where he resides with his wife and three children.

Robert Cording - Robert Cording has published nine collections of poems, the most recent of which are *Only So Far* (CavanKerry Press, 2015) and *Without My Asking* (CavanKerry Press, 2019). A new book on poetry, the Bible, and metaphor, *Finding the World's Fullness*, is out from Slant. He has received two NEAs in poetry and two fellowships in poetry from the Connecticut Arts Association. He has won a Pushcart Prize in poetry, and his poems have appeared in publications such as the *Georgia Review*, *Southern Review*, *Poetry*, *Hudson Review*, *Kenyon Review*, *New Ohio Review*, *Orion*, *Agni*, and *Best American Poetry 2018*.

Sam Cornish - Sam Cornish grew up in Baltimore, MD and lived in Boston, MA until his death in 2018. Following his move to Boston, he was a teacher at the Highland Park Community School in Roxbury, MA, and was also active in the Poetry in the Schools Program in Boston and Cambridge, MA. In the early 80s, he was the literature director of the Massachusetts Council on the Arts and Humanities and subsequently, an instructor in creative writing at Emerson College until his retirement in 2006. In addition to his nine books of poetry and two children's books, his work has been published in dozens of periodicals, including *Essence, Ploughshares, Harvard Review*, the *Christian Science Monitor*, and the *Boston Globe*. In 2007, he was chosen as the first Poet Laureate of the City of Boston.

Paola Corso - Paola Corso is the author of seven poetry and fiction books set in her native Pittsburgh where her Italian immigrant family found work in the steel mills. Her nonfiction has appeared in venues such as the *New York Times*, *Women's Review of Books*, and *U.S. Catholic*. Writing honors include a New York Foundation for the Arts Poetry Fellowship and Sherwood Anderson

Fiction Prize, as well as inclusion on Pennsylvania Center for the Book's Cultural and Literary Map. A literary activist, Corso is cofounder and resident artist of Steppin Stanzas, a poetry and art project celebrating city steps. She is a member of Park Slope Windsor Terrace Artists Collective, who exhibits her photographs in libraries, galleries, and open studios. She divides her time between New York City, where she is on the English department faculty at Touro College, and Pittsburgh. paolacorso.com

Shira Dentz - Shira Dentz is the author of two chapbooks and five books including *Sisyphusina* (PANK, 2020), *door of thin skins* (CavanKerry Press, 2013), and *how do I net thee* (Salmon Poetry, 2018), a National Poetry Series finalist. Her writing appears in many venues including *Poetry*, *American Poetry Review*, *New American Writing*, *Iowa Review*, Academy of American Poets' Poem-a-Day series (Poets.org), and NPR. A recipient of awards including an Academy of American Poets' Prize, Poetry Society of America's Lyric Poem Award, and Poetry Society of America's Cecil Hemley Memorial Award, she is special features editor at Tarpaulin Sky and teaches in upstate NY. More about her writing can be found at www.shiradentz.com

Moyra Donaldson - Moyra Donaldson is from Northern Ireland. She has published nine collections of poetry, including a limited-edition publication of artwork and poems, *Blood Horses*, in collaboration with artist Paddy Lennon. Her most recent collection is *Carnivorous* (Doire Press, 2019). In 2019, she received a Major Individual Artist award from Arts Council NI.

Catherine Doty - Catherine Doty is a poet and educator from Paterson, New Jersey. She is the author of *momentum* (CavanKerry Press, 2004), a collection of poems. She has received fellowships and prizes from the National Endowment for the Arts, the New York Foundation for the Arts, the New Jersey State Council on the Arts, and the Academy of American Poets.

Sherry Fairchok - Sherry Fairchok was born in Scranton in 1962. She spent the early part of her childhood in Taylor, PA, a coal-mining town, in which her family has lived since the 1880s, and where her grandfather, great-uncles, and great-grandfather worked as miners. She earned a bachelor's degree from Syracuse University and an MFA degree from Sarah Lawrence College. Her poems have appeared in the *Southern Review*, *Ploughshares*, *DoubleTake*, and *Poetry*

Northwest, among other journals. She works as an information technology editor and lives in Mount Vernon, NY.

Marie Lawson Fiala - Marie Lawson Fiala, born in Europe, came to the United States as a child. Her first language was Czech, and she learned English only after starting grade school. She earned her bachelor of arts degree in psychology with distinction from Stanford University, her juris doctor degree from Stanford Law School, and her master of fine arts in writing from the University of San Francisco. She is a full-time practicing attorney and a partner in an international law firm, specializing in complex commercial litigation.

Sondra Gash - Sondra Gash grew up in Paterson, NJ. Her poems have appeared in the *New York Times*, *Calyx*, the *Paterson Literary Review*, and *U.S. 1 Worksheets*. She has received grants from the New Jersey State Council on the Arts and the Corporation of Yaddo, and won first prize in the Allen Ginsberg Poetry Competition. In 1999, the Geraldine Dodge Foundation awarded her a fellowship to the Virginia Center for the Arts. She lives with her husband in New Jersey, where she teaches writing and directs the poetry program at the Women's Resource Center in Summit.

Ross Gay - Ross Gay was born in Youngstown, Ohio, and grew up outside of Philadelphia. His poems have appeared in *American Poetry Review*, *Harvard Review*, and *Atlanta Review*, among other journals. Ross is a Cave Canem fellow and has been a Breadloaf Tuition Scholar. In addition to holding a PhD in American literature from Temple University, he is a basketball coach, an occasional demolition man, and a painter, and teaches at Indiana University.

Loren Graham - Loren Graham was raised in and around Broken Arrow, Oklahoma. He studied as a writer and composer at Oklahoma Baptist University, Baylor University, and the University of Virginia. He received a National Endowment for the Arts Fellowship in 2009 for poems that became part of *Places I Was Dreaming*. He currently lives in Helena, Montana, with his wife, Jane Shawn.

John Haines - John Haines, poet, essayist, and teacher, was born in 1924 and died in March 2011. After studying painting, he spent more than twenty years homesteading in Alaska. The author of more than ten collections of poetry, his works include *At the End of This Summer: Poems 1948–1954*, *The Owl* *in the Mask of the Dreamer, and New Poems 1980–88*, for which he received both the Lenore Marshall Poetry Prize and the Western States Book Award. He taught at Ohio University, George Washington University, University of Montana, Bucknell University, and the University of Cincinnati. He was a resident at the Rockefeller Center, Bellagio, Italy, and the Rasmuson Fellow at the US Artists Meeting, Los Angeles. Named a fellow by the Academy of American Poets in 1997, his other honors include the Alaska Governor's Award for Excellence in the Arts, two Guggenheim Fellowships, an Amy Lowell Traveling Fellowship, a National Endowment for the Arts Fellowship, and a Lifetime Achievement Award from the Library of Congress. In 2008, *Sewanee Review* awarded Haines the Atkin Taylor Award for Poetry.

Joan Cusack Handler - As the founder of CavanKerry Press, Joan is a poet and memoirist, a psychologist, and a blogger for PsychologyToday.com ("Of Art and Science"). Her widely published poems have received the Sampler Award from the *Boston Review* and five Pushcart nominations. She has four books. Three are poetry, *GlOrious*, *The Red Canoe: Love in Its Making*, and *Orphans*; and one is memoir, *Confessions of Joan the Tall*. A Bronx native, she currently lives in Brooklyn and East Hampton, New York.

Judith Hannan - Judith Hannan is the author of *Motherhood Exaggerated* (CavanKerry Press, 2012), her memoir of discovery and transformation during her daughter's cancer treatment and transition into survival. Her most recent book is *The Write Prescription: Telling Your Story to Live With and Beyond Illness.* Her essays have appeared in such publications as the *Washington Post*, *AARP*, the *Girlfriend, Woman's Day, Narratively*, the *Forward, Brevity, Opera News*, the *Healing Muse*, and the *Martha's Vineyard Gazette*. Judith Hannan teaches writing about personal experience to homeless mothers and young women in the criminal justice system as well as to those affected by physical and/or mental illness. She is a writing mentor with the Memorial Sloan-Kettering Cancer Center's Visible Ink program where she also serves as an interventionist in a study to evaluate the benefits of expressive writing among elderly cancer patients. In June 2016, she joined the faculty of the inaugural Narrative Medicine Program at Kripalu. In 2015, she received a Humanism-in-Medicine award from the Arnold P. Gold Foundation. Judith Hannan serves on the board of the Children's Museum of Manhattan where she is also Writer-in-Residence. www.judithhannanwrites.com

Elizabeth Hall Hutner – Elizabeth Hall Hutner was a writer, scholar, and musician who lived in Princeton, N.J., where she completed her PhD in comparative literature at Princeton University. Her short essays have been published in *A Real Life*, a bimonthly magazine. Hutner graduated from Yale University, where she studied with Mark Strand and J.D. McClatchy, and she worked with Marvin Bell at the Breadloaf Writers' Conference. She also held a master of arts from Princeton. She died of breast cancer in November, 2002.

Susan Jackson - Susan Jackson is a New Jersey poet now living in Teton County, Wyoming. CavanKerry Press published her first poetry collection, *Through a Gate of Trees*, in 2007. Jackson's work has been published in numerous journals and literary magazines. She is grateful to CKP for the press's dedication to the power of literature to explore the depths of human experience.

Marcus Jackson - Marcus Jackson was born in Toledo, Ohio. His poetry has appeared in the *New Yorker*, *Harvard Review*, *Cincinnati Review*, and *Hayden's Ferry Review*, among many other publications. He has received fellowships from New York University and Cave Canem.

Gray Jacobik - Gray Jacobik is a widely anthologized poet; *The Double Task* was selected by James Tate for the Juniper Prize; *The Surface of Last Scattering* received the X. J. Kennedy Prize; *Brave Disguises*, the AWP Poetry Series Award. In 2016 *The Banquet: New & Selected Poems* received the William Meredith Award in Poetry. She's been awarded the Yeats Prize, the Emily Dickinson Award, and the *Third Coast* Poetry Prize. Jacobik is a painter as well as a poet and several CKP covers have featured her art. http://www.grayjacobik.com/

David Keller - David Keller is the author of five collections of poetry. He has taught poetry workshops in New York and has served as poetry coordinator for the Geraldine R. Dodge Biennial Poetry Festival, on the Board of Governors for the Poetry Society of America, and as a member of the advisory board of the Frost Place.

Tina Kelley - Tina Kelley's fourth poetry collection, *Rise Wildly,* was released in 2020 from CavanKerry Press, which also published *Abloom & Awry* (2017). *Ardor* won the Jacar Press 2017 chapbook competition. Her other books are *Precise* (Word Press, 2013), and *The Gospel of Galore,* winner of a 2003

Washington State Book Award. She coauthored *Almost Home: Helping Kids Move from Homelessness to Hope,* and was a reporter for the *New York Times* for a decade, sharing in a staff Pulitzer for coverage of the 9/11 attacks. She wrote 121 "Portraits of Grief," short descriptions of the victims, and many stories about oppression: the health problems of a Native American tribe living near a Superfund site, a high school student who challenged a proselytizing public school teacher and who received a death threat for his stance, a transgender vocational school principal in a rural town, and the lives of children waiting to be adopted out of foster care. Her journalism has appeared in *Orion*, *Audubon*, and *People*, and her poetry has appeared in *Poetry East*, *North American Review*, *Poetry Northwest*, *Prairie Schooner*, *Best American Poetry*, and on the buses of Seattle. She and her husband have two children and live in Maplewood, NJ.

Christine Korfhage - Christine Korfhage was born in Albany, NY and grew up overseas. A former artisan and juried member of the League of New Hampshire Craftsmen, she began writing poetry at age 49. Returning to school after three decades, in 1999 she received her BA from Vermont College's Adult Degree Program where she was awarded a fellowship for excellence in creative writing. She received her MFA from Bennington College in 2001. Her poems have appeared in many journals, including *Chiron Review*, *Connecticut River Review*, *Nimrod International Review*, *Paterson Literary Review*, *Pearl*, *Red Rock Review*, and the *Spoon River Poetry Review*. A mother and grandmother, Christine lives in New Hampshire.

Laurie Lamon - Laurie Lamon's poems have appeared in journals and magazines including the *Atlantic*, the *New Republic*, *Arts & Letters Journal of Contemporary Culture*, *Plume*, *Ploughshares*, *J Journal: New Writing on Justice*, *Innisfree Poetry Journal*, *North American Review*, and others. She was the recipient of a Pushcart Prize and was selected by Donald Hall as a Witter Bynner Fellow in 2007. She currently holds the Amy Ryan Endowed Professorship at Whitworth University in Spokane, Washington, and is poetry editor for the literary journal *Rock & Sling*. She lives with her husband Bill Siems, and their two dachshund Chihuahua dogs, Willow and Johnny.

Joseph O. Legaspi - Joseph O. Legaspi is the author of the poetry collections *Threshold* and *Imago,* both from CavanKerry Press, and three chapbooks: *Post-*

cards (Ghost Bird Press, 2019), *Aviary, Bestiary* (Organic Weapon Arts, 2014), and *Subways* (Thrush Press, 2013). He cofounded Kundiman (www.kundiman.org), a non-profit organization serving generations of writers and readers of Asian American literature.

Harriet Levin - Harriet Levin is the author of *The Christmas Show* (Beacon Press, 1997), winner of the Barnard New Women Poets Prize and the Poetry Society of America's Alice Fay di Castagnola Award; *Girl in Cap and Gown* (Mammoth Books, 2010), a National Poetry Series finalist; and *My Oceanography* (CavanKerry, 2018). Her novel, *How Fast Can You Run* (Harvard Square Editions, 2016), grew out of a One Book, One Philadelphia writing project from interviews with Sudanese refugee Michael Majok Kuch and was excerpted in the *Kenyon Review*. She holds an MFA from the University of Iowa and teaches writing at Drexel University.

Howard Levy - Howard Levy is the author of CavanKerry's first book, *A Day This Lit*. His work has appeared in *Poetry, Threepenny Review*, and the *Gettysburg Review*. He has served as a faculty member of the Frost Place Poetry Festival and currently lives in New York.

Frannie Lindsay - *The Snow's Wife* is Frannie Lindsay's sixth volume. Previous work appears in the *Atlantic Monthly*, the *American Poetry Review*, the *Yale Review, Field, Plume,* and *Best American Poetry*. She has held fellowships from the National Endowment for the Arts and the Massachusetts Cultural Council. She teaches workshops on grief and trauma.

Christopher Matthews - Christopher Matthews was born in Donegal, Ireland and grew up and was educated between that country and England. He took his bachelor's degree at the University of Ulster and obtained a PhD from the University of Durham: its subject was Ezra Pound. His poems have appeared in the *American Scholar, Crazyhorse, Dublin Review,* and other journals. He currently teaches literature to undergraduates in Lugano, Switzerland.

Michael Miller - Michael Miller's *Darkening the Grass* is the third book by an accomplished American poet who is in his eighth decade. *The Joyful Dark*, his first book, was the "Editor's Choice" winner of the McGovern Prize at Ashland Poetry Press. His poems have appeared in the *Kenyon Review, Sewanee Review,*

American Scholar, *New Republic, Raritan*, *Southern Review*, *Yale Review*, and other publications. Born in New York City in 1940, he now lives in Massachusetts.

Martin Mooney - Martin Mooney's poetry, short fiction, reviews, criticism, and cultural commentary have been published in Irish and British periodicals. Following *Grub*, which on its original release in Ireland won the Brendan Behand Memorial Award, Mooney published *Bonfire Makers*, *Operation Sandcastle*, and *Rasputin and His Children*. His poems have appeared in *Field* and *Gettsyburg Review*. He was writer-in-residence at the Brighton Festival and the Aspects Festival of Irish Writing, and twice was appointed a member of the resident faculty at the Robert Frost Place Poetry Festival in Franconia, NH.

Mark Nepo - Mark Nepo has moved and inspired readers and seekers all over the world. Beloved as a poet, teacher, and storyteller, Mark has been called "one of the finest spiritual guides of our time." A #1 *New York Times* bestselling author, his twenty-two books and fifteen audio projects have been translated into over twenty languages.

Richard Jeffrey Newman - Richard Jeffrey Newman, an associate professor at Nassau Community College, New York, is an essayist, poet, and translator who has been publishing his work since 1988, when the essay "His Sexuality; Her Reproductive Rights" appeared in *Changing Men* magazine. Since then, his essays, poems, and translations have appeared in a wide range of journals, among them *Prairie Schooner* and *Birmingham Poetry Review.* He has given talks and led workshops on writing autobiographically about gender, sex, and sexuality.

Brent Newsom - Brent Newsom is the author of *Love's Labors* (CavanKerry Press, 2015) and the librettist for *A Porcelain Doll,* an opera based on the life of deafblind pioneer Laura Bridgman. His poems have also appeared in *Southern Review*, *Hopkins Review*, *Cave Wall*, and other journals. He lives and teaches in central Oklahoma.

Kari O'Driscoll - Kari is a writer and mother of two living in the Pacific Northwest. Her work has appeared in print anthologies on mothering, reproductive rights, and cancer, as well as online in outlets such as Ms. Magazine, ParentMap, The ManifestStation, and Healthline. She is the founder of The SELF Project, an organization whose goals are to help teenagers, teachers, and caregivers of teens recognize the unique challenges and amazing attributes of adolescents and to use mindfulness and nonviolent communication to build better relationships. You can find her at www.kariodriscollwriter.com.

January Gill O'Neil - January Gill O'Neil is the executive director of the Massachusetts Poetry Festival, an assistant professor of English at Salem State University, and a board of trustees' member with the Association of Writers and Writing Programs (AWP) and Montserrat College of Art. A Cave Canem fellow, January's poems and articles have appeared in the *New York Times Magazine*, former US Poet Laureate Tracy K. Smith's podcast "The Slowdown," the Academy of American Poet's Poem-A-Day series, *American Poetry Review*, *New England Review*, and *Ploughshares*, among others. In 2018, January was awarded a Massachusetts Cultural Council grant, and is the John and Renée Grisham Writer in Residence for 2019–2020 at the University of Mississippi, Oxford.

Georgianna Orsini - Georgianna Orsini attended Wellesley College and Harvard University and received her BA degree from Columbia University, during which time she worked as a program coordinator at International House. She has lived in Tuscany and New York. Her gardens have been featured in *House and Garden, House Beautiful*, and *American Women's Garden*. At present, she lives in the mountains of North Carolina where she continues to make gardens.

Adriana Páramo - Adrianna Páramo is a Colombian anthropologist and winner of the Social Justice and Equality Award in creative nonfiction with her book *Looking for Esperanza*. Her writing has appeared in *Alaska Quarterly Review*, *Los Angeles Review*, *Consequence Magazine*, *Fourteen Hills*, *Carolina Quarterly Review*, *Magnolia Journal*, *So To Speak*, *Compass Rose*, and *Phati'tude,* among others. Páramo has volunteered her time as a transcriber for *Voice of Witness*, a book series which empowers those affected by social injustice.

Peggy Penn - Peggy Penn's poetry has appeared in several publications including *O Magazine*, the *Paris Review*, *Beloit Poetry Journal*, *Western Humanities Review*, *Southern Poetry Review*, and *Margie Review*. She won the poem for the first poem published in the journal *Kimera*, and the first Emily Dickinson Award for innovative poetry.

Donald Platt - Donald Platt's fifth book, *Tornadoesque*, appeared through CavanKerry Press's Notable Voices series in 2016. His sixth book, *Man Praying*, was published by Parlor Press / Free Verse Editions in 2017. He is a recipient of two fellowships from the National Endowment for the Arts and three Pushcart Prizes. Currently, he is a full professor of English at Purdue University.

Cati Porter - Cati Porter is a poet, editor, essayist, arts administrator, wife, mother, daughter, friend. She is the author of eight books and chapbooks, and her poems have appeared in Verse Daily, *Contrary*, *West Trestle Review*, *So to Speak*, the *Nervous Breakdown*, and others, as well as many anthologies. Her personal essays have appeared in Salon, The Manifest-Station, and Zocalo Public Square. She is founder and editor of *Poemeleon: A Journal of Poetry*, established in 2005. She lives in Riverside, California, with her family where she directs Inlandia Institute, a literary nonprofit.

Dawn Potter - Dawn Potter is the author of eight books of prose and poetry. New work appears in the *Beloit Poetry Journal*, the *Split Rock Review*, *Vox Populi*, and many other journals. She has received fellowships and awards from the Elizabeth George Foundation, the Writers' Center, and the Maine Arts Commission, and her memoir *Tracing Paradise* won the Maine Literary Award in Nonfiction. Dawn directs the Frost Place Conference on Poetry and Teaching and leads the high school writing seminars at Monson Arts. She lives in Portland, Maine.

Wanda S. Praisner - Wanda S. Praisner is the recipient of the Egan Award, Princemere Prize, Kudzu Award, First Prize in Poetry at the College of NJ Writers' Conference, and the 2017 New Jersey Poets Prize. Her work appears in *Atlanta Review*, *Lullwater Review*, and *Prairie Schooner*. Her sixth collection is *To Illuminate the Way* (Aldrich Press, 2018). She's a resident poet for the state of New Jersey.

Jack Ridl - Jack Ridl is the author of several collections of poetry, including *Broken Symmetry*, *Outside the Center Ring*, and *Against Elegies*, and several literature textbooks. He taught poetry and literature for thirty-six years, was named one of the 100 most influential educators in the world of sport by the Institute for International Sport, and awarded Michigan Professor of the Year by CASE and the Carnegie Foundation. He learned about basketball from his father, Hall of Fame basketball coach C.G. "Buzz" Ridl.

Kenneth Rosen - Kenneth Rosen was born in Boston, and has lived in Maine since 1965. He recently taught at the American University in Bulgaria, and as a Fulbright professor at Sofia University. *Whole Horse*, his first collection, was selected for Richard Howard's Braziller Poetry Series. Others are *The Hebrew Lion*, *Black Leaves*, *Longfellow Square*, *Reptile Mind*, and *No Snake, No Paradise*. He founded the Stonecoast Writers' Conference in 1981, and directed it for ten years.

Mary Ruefle – Mary Ruefle has published several books of poetry, including *Among the Musk Ox People* (Carnegie Mellon, 2002). *Apparition Hill* was completed in 1989 in China, where she was teaching. It falls between her books, *The Adamant* (University of Iowa, 1989) and *Cold Pluto* (Carnegie Mellon, 1996). She is the recipient of a National Endowment for the Arts Creative Fellowship, a Whiting Writers' Award, and an Award in Literature from the American Academy of Arts and Letters. She teaches in the MFA in Writing Program at Vermont College.

Maureen Seaton - Maureen Seaton has authored numerous poetry collections, solo and collaborative. Her awards include the Lambda Literary, NEA, and Pushcart. Her memoir, *Sex Talks to Girls* (University of Wisconsin, 2008, 2018), also garnered a "Lammy." Seaton is a professor of creative writing at the University of Miami.

Robert Seder – Robert Seder was a production and lighting designer for many dance and theater companies for twenty years, working with David Gordon, Lucinda Childs, Meredith Monk, Carolyn Brown, Eric Bogosian, and Philip Glass, among others. He was a semifinalist for the Julie Harris Playwright award in 1987 with LIGHT, and wrote several other plays, produced in New York City, Madison, and Boston. He also wrote novels and short stories in addition to his narrative of his first bone marrow transplant. He was an enthusiastic participant and teacher in the Bard College Language and Thinking Program and also offered "Writing Our Illness" workshops to the community. After undergoing a second bone marrow transplant in August 2001, he died on March 6,

2002, from multiple infections that his weakened immune system was unable to defeat.

Fred Shaw - Fred Shaw is a graduate of the University of Pittsburgh, and Carlow University, where he received his MFA. He teaches writing and literature at Point Park University and Carlow University. His first collection, *Scraping Away,* was published by CavanKerry Press in Spring 2020. He is also a book reviewer and poetry editor for *Pittsburgh Quarterly*. His poem "Argot" is featured in the 2018 full-length documentary *Eating & Working & Eating & Working*, a film focusing on the lives of local service-industry workers. His poem "Scraping Away" was selected for the PA Public Poetry Project in 2017. He lives in Pittsburgh with his wife and rescued hound dog.

Danny Shot - Danny Shot was longtime publisher and editor of *Long Shot* magazine, which he founded along with Eliot Katz. His poems and stories have been widely anthologized, and he's performed his work everywhere. He lives in Hoboken, NJ (home of Frank Sinatra and baseball). He was featured in the widely acclaimed TV show *State of the Arts*. His play *Roll the Dice* was produced in September 2018 as part of the New York Theater Festival. Danny currently serves as Head Poetry Editor of Red Fez online magazine (https://www.redfez.net/).

Joan Seliger Sidney - Joan Seliger Sidney is writer-in-residence at the University of Connecticut's Center for Judaic Studies and Contemporary Jewish Life. She also facilitates "Writing for Your Life," an adult writing workshop. Her dream-came-true job was teaching creative writing at the Université de Grenoble, France. Her poems have appeared in *Michigan Quarterly Review*, *Massachusetts Review*, *Louisville Review*, *Kaleidoscope*, and *Anthology of Magazine Verse & Yearbook of American Poetry*. She has received fellowships from the Connecticut Commission on the Arts, the Christopher Reeve Paralysis Foundation, and the Vermont Studio Center. Her poems published in 2003 were nominated for a Pushcart Prize XXIX. She lives in Storrs, Connecticut, with her husband. Their four adult children are thriving.

Robin Silbergleid - Robin Silbergleid is the author of several books and chapbooks, including *In the Cubiculum Nocturnum* (Dancing Girl Press, 2019) and the memoir *Texas Girl* (Demeter Press, 2014); she is also coeditor of *Reading and Writing Experimental Texts: Critical Innovations* (Palgrave, 2017).

Currently, she lives in East Lansing, Michigan, where she teaches and directs the Creative Writing Program at Michigan State University. Her collection *The Baby Book* was published by CKP in 2015.

Judith Sornberger - Judith Sornberger's poetry books are *Practicing the World* (CavanKerry Press, 2018), *I Call to You from Time* (Wipf & Stock, 2019), and *Open Heart* (Calyx Books, 1993). She is also the author of five chapbooks, most recently *Wal-Mart Orchid* (Evening Street Press, 2011), and a prose memoir, *The Accidental Pilgrim: Finding God and His Mother in Tuscany* (Shanti Arts Press, 2015).

Sarah Sousa – Sarah Sousa is the author of the poetry collections *See the Wolf*, named a 2019 "Must Read" book by the Massachusetts Center for the Book, *Split the Crow*, and *Church of Needles*. Her poems have appeared in the *Massachusetts Review*, *North American Review*, the *Southern Poetry Review*, *Verse Daily*, and *Tupelo Quarterly*, among others. Her honors include a Dorothy Sargent Rosenberg Fellowship and a Massachusetts Cultural Council Fellowship. She is a member of the board of directors of Perugia Press.

Margo Taft Stever - In 2019, CavanKerry Press published Margo Taft Stever's *Cracked Piano*, and Kattywompus Press published her chapbook *Ghost Moose*. She is the founder of the Hudson Valley Writers Center and founding editor of Slapering Hol Press. She teaches poetry to at-risk children at Children's Village. For more information, please see: www.margotaftstever.com.

Carole Stone – Carole Stone is the author of two books of poetry and seven chapbooks as well as many critical essays on writers, among them George Eliot, Edna St. Vincent Millay, and Sylvia Plath. A recipient of fellowships from the NJ State Council on the Arts and residencies at Hawthornden Castle International Retreat for Writers in Scotland and Chateau de Lavigny in Switzerland, she is professor of English emerita, Montclair State University. She divides her time between New Jersey and East Hampton, N.Y.

Cindy Veach - Cindy Veach is the author of *Her Kind* (CavanKerry Press, forthcoming) and *Gloved Against Blood* (CavanKerry Press, 2017), named a finalist for the Paterson Poetry Prize and a "Must Read" by the Massachusetts Center for the Book. Her poems have appeared in the Academy of American Poets

Poem-a-Day Series, *AGNI*, *Prairie Schooner*, *Poet Lore*, *Michigan Quarterly Review*, *Diode*, and elsewhere. She received the 2019 Phillip Booth Poetry Prize and the 2018 Samuel Allen Washington Prize. www.cindyveach.com

Phoebe Sparrow Wagner - Artist, poet, coauthor of *Divided Minds: Twin Sisters and their Journey through Schizophrenia* (St. Martin's Press, 2005) and author of *We Mad Climb Shaky Ladders* (CavanKerry Press, 2009). Her third book, poems and original art, *Learning to See in Three Dimensions* (Green Writers Press, 2017), is now also available from Amazon and other booksellers. Visit http://phoebesparrowwagner.com for Wagner's poetry.

Sarah Bracey White - A southerner transplanted to New York, Sarah Bracey White mines her past in memoir, essays, and poetry. She is the author of *Primary Lessons*; *The Wanderlust*, a folk tale; and *Feelings Brought to Surface*, a poetry collection. She is a frequent contributor to Read 650, the literary performance group. Visit her website www.onmymind.org for more information.

Jack Wiler - Jack Wiler was raised in New Jersey and lived in Jersey City until his death in 2009. Diagnosed with AIDS in 2001, Jack spent the last years of his life writing and educating students about poetry. For much of his life, he worked in pest control, most notably for Acme Exterminating in New York. He worked for *Long Shot Magazine* for many years and in association with the Geraldine R. Dodge Foundation worked as a visiting poet in the schools. Jack's words can be found online at http://jackwiler.blogspot.com.

Baron Wormser - Baron Wormser is the author of eighteen books. Wormser has received fellowships from the National Endowment for the Arts and the John Simon Guggenheim Memorial Foundation. From 2000 to 2005 he served as poet laureate of the state of Maine.

CAVANKERRY'S BOOKS

2000	A Day This Lit	Howard Levy
	Kazimierz Square	Karen Chase
2001	Carolyn Kizer: Perspectives on Her Life & Work	Annie Finch, Johanna Keller, and Candace McClelland, Editors
	The Breath of Parted Lips: Voices from the Robert Frost Place, Volume I	Donald Hall (Foreword)
	So Close	Peggy Penn
2002	Against Consolation	Robert Cording
	Grub	Martin Mooney
	Apparition Hill	Mary Ruefle
	Snakeskin Stilettos	Moyra Donaldson
	Silk Elegy	Sondra Gash
2003	The Palace of Ashes	Sherry Fairchok
	A Gradual Twilight: An Appreciation of John Haines	Steven B. Rogers, Editor
	The Origins of Tragedy & Other Poems	Kenneth Rosen
	GlOrious	Joan Cusack Handler
	Eyelevel: Fifty Histories	Christopher Matthews
2004	Rattle	Eloise Bruce
	Soft Box	Celia Bland
	An Imperfect Lover	Georgianna Orsini
	The Breath of Parted Lips: Voices from the Robert Frost Place, Volume II	Sydney Lea, Editor
	momentum	Catherine Doty
	Body of Diminishing Motion	Joan Seliger Sidney
	Life with Sam	Elizabeth Hall Hutner

2005	The Singers I Prefer	Christian Barter
	The Fork Without Hunger	Laurie Lamon
2006	The Disheveled Bed	Andrea Carter Brown
	Common Life	Robert Cording
	The Silence of Men	Richard Jeffrey Newman
	Fun Being Me	Jack Wiler
	Against Which	Ross Gay
2007	Surviving Has Made Me Crazy	Mark Nepo
	To the Marrow	Robert Seder
	Through a Gate of Trees	Susan Jackson
	Imago	Joseph O. Legaspi
	We Aren't Who We Are and this world isn't either	Christine Korfhage
2008	Elegy for the Floater	Teresa Carson
	BEAR	Karen Chase
	The Poetry Life: Ten Stories	Baron Wormser
	An Apron Full of Beans: New and Selected Poems	Sam Cornish
	Red Canoe: Love In Its Making	Joan Cusack Handler
2009	We Mad Climb Shaky Ladders	Phoebe Sparrow Wagner
	The Second Night of the Spirit	Bhisham Bherwani
	Without Wings	Laurie Lamon
	Losing Season	Jack Ridl
	Southern Comfort	Nin Andrews
	Underlife	January Gill O'Neil
2010	The Waiting Room Reader, Volume I	Joan Cusack Handler, Editor
	Descent	John Haines
	Letters from a Distant Shore	Marie Lawson Fiala
	How the Crimes Happened	Dawn Potter
	Divina Is Divina	Jack Wiler
	Walking with Ruskin	Robert Cording
2011	Little Boy Blue: A Memoir in Verse	Gray Jacobik
	Impenitent Notes	Baron Wormser

CAVANKERRY'S MISSION

A not-for-profit literary press serving art and community, CavanKerry is committed to expanding the reach of poetry and other fine literature to a general readership by publishing works that explore the emotional and psychological landscapes of everyday life, and to bringing that art to the underserved where they live, work, and receive services.

This book was printed on paper from responsible sources.

This collection has been set in FreightSans Pro, the sans serif counterpart to the typeface FreightText. The humanist forms of FreightSans Pro give it a warm and friendly appearance. It was designed by Joshua Darden and published by GarageFonts in 2009.